Dear Heart

Dear Heart

150 New Zealand Love Poems
Paula Green (editor)

GODWIT

Contents

Introduction	11
Dream — *Brian Turner*	17
Arohanui — *Robert Sullivan*	18
Love in the Early Winter — *Jenny Powell*	19
Wedding song — *Jenny Bornholdt*	20
The Apple Picker — *Sarah Jane Barnett*	22
Love poem — *Gregory O'Brien*	23
Apartment — *Virginia Were*	24
Son — *Angela Andrews*	25
Love Poem for a Love a Long Time Ago — *Airini Beautrais*	26
Audrey — *Charles Spear*	27
[but you . . .] — *Wystan Curnow*	28
Love Poem for the Tauherenikau River — *Airini Beautrais*	29
The Verb to Give — *Dinah Hawken*	30
The Beach House — *James K Baxter*	32
talk about a tonic — *Diane Brown*	33
Glenburn — *Paula Green*	34
Wild Daisies — *Bub Bridger*	35
wedding song — *Bernadette Hall*	36
Ruby's heirloom dress — *Elizabeth Smither*	37
The castle — *Fiona Farrell*	38
keeping warm — *Michele Leggott*	40
Love Song — *Rachel McAlpine*	44

Brightness — *Denis Glover*	45
Inesilla — *Bill Manhire*	46
Billet-doux — *Michael Harlow*	48
Love by Candlelight — *Mary Stanley*	49
To Utopias — *Ian Wedde*	50
Tipple Over Tail — *Johanna Emeney*	52
You — *C K Stead*	53
grahams beach, bach — *Sonja Yelich*	54
The Miracle — *Jack Ross*	55
Bear Dance — *Peter Bland*	56
For the father of my children — *Karlo Mila*	58
The Wish — *Kevin Ireland*	60
Husband to Wife — *Chris Tse*	61
Great Full Moon, Lowering Behind the Black Hill	
— *Anna Livesey*	62
Poem for Kereihi — *Hone Tuwhare*	63
At the Beginning of Love — *Elizabeth Smither*	64
Child — *Janet Frame*	65
Words and Roses *from* Cages For the Wind	
— *Alistair Te Ariki Campbell*	67
If She Hadn't Been There — *Brian Turner*	69
A Late Honeymoon — *Iain Lonie*	70
The ngaio tree — *Fiona Kidman*	72
Puriri — *Jan Kemp*	74
Before I Get into Sleep with You — *Janet Frame*	75
Embrace — *Robin Hyde*	76
Life eternal — *Diana Bridge*	77
Time of Day — *Hinemoana Baker*	78
His eyes — *Joanna Margaret Paul*	79
I love peaches — *Vivienne Plumb*	80
Traveller overdue — *Emma Neale*	81
lovesong — *Bernadette Hall*	82

because — *Sarah Broom*	83
My Mother's Voice — *Ingrid Horrocks*	84
White Gold — *Jenny Powell*	85
Fontanello — *Anna Jackson*	86
Still Life — *Joanna Margaret Paul*	87
A Lightning Tree — *Cilla McQueen*	88
The nervous public speaker — *Lauris Edmond*	90
Puer Natus — *Mary Stanley*	91
The Sounds — *Andrew Johnston*	92
A Letter — *David Mitchell*	94
Quarantine Island — *Harry Ricketts*	95
A new plateau song — *Sam Hunt*	96
As big as a father — *Jeffrey Paparoa Holman*	98
Inventing You — *Kevin Ireland*	100
The Language of Bluff — *Cilla McQueen*	102
Husband and Wife Talk Without Talking at a Difficult Dinner Party — *Joan Fleming*	103
After Apollinaire — *Jack Ross*	104
from dia — *Michele Leggott*	106
Returned Memory — *Dinah Hawken*	107
The treehouse — *Anna Jackson*	108
Change — *A R D Fairburn*	110
Seven wishes — *Fiona Farrell*	111
A Consort of Flower Parts — *Gregory O'Brien*	112
Found Again — *Serie Barford*	116
Birdsong — *Sarah Broom*	118
to Pru — *Apirana Taylor*	120
Urgently — *J C Sturm*	121
Calculations — *Kapka Kassabova*	122
Letter home — *Sam Hunt*	123
Love Affair — *Riemke Ensing*	124
The photograph — *Alison Wong*	125

Ending and going home — *Jenny Bornholdt*	126
Watching the Motorway by Moonlight — *Iain Sharp*	127
warm loaf — *Janet Charman*	128
My Mother Dances — *Albert Wendt*	129
Love poem for David — *Selina Tusitala Marsh*	130
Twelve Words Spoken by a Poem — *Jill Chan*	133
from Treasure Hunt — *Mike Johnson*	135
The Voyage — *Bill Manhire*	137
See what a little moonlight can do to you? — *Hone Tuwhare*	138
Tell me you're waiting — *Peter Bland*	139
Free fall — *Harry Ricketts*	140
Coming and Going — *Louis Johnson*	141
The Bicycle — *James Brown*	142
Between — *Rhian Gallagher*	144
viaduct — *Jen Crawford*	145
At your visit — *Joanna Margaret Paul*	146
The Dance — *Rhian Gallagher*	147
you are a hot -concentrate — *Janet Charman*	148
December — *Sarah Quigley*	150
Dog's body — *Chris Price*	151
Mute song — *Kate Camp*	152
Picnic at Darkness Falls — *James Brown*	154
Remembering Summer — *Brian Turner*	156
The gift — *Peter Bland*	157
This is Love — *Karlo Mila*	159
The Tides Run Up the Wairau — *Eileen Duggan*	161
Lemon Tree — *Owen Marshall*	162
Portland Crescent — *Anna Smaill*	163
from The Bond Of Time: An Epic Love Poem — *John Puhiatau Pule*	164
Deserts, for instance — *Brian Turner*	166
A Lullaby — *Bill Manhire*	167

A Girl's Song — *Ruth Dallas*	168
Homage — *Ursula Bethell*	169
The Grin — *Keith Sinclair*	171
from In Your Presence — *Charles Brasch*	172
Cassino *Città Martire* — *Robert Sullivan*	174
Bouquet of Dead Flowers — *David Eggleton*	176
Of books and bookcases — *Kiri Piahana-Wong*	177
The Fire is Lovely — *Richard Langston*	179
the bird — *Glenn Colquhoun*	180
He Waiata mo Te Kare — *James K Baxter*	183
Lyric — *Michael Steven*	190
light — *Alison Wong*	191
Aunty Huia — *Glenn Colquhoun*	192
The Inner Life — *Jenny Bornholdt*	194
Love in the Jam-maker's Mansion — *James Norcliffe*	195
Wide open spaces — *Lynn Davidson*	196
At Scorching Bay — *Bernadette Hall*	197
Barbara — *Bob Orr*	198
Love in the Dark Country — *Kapka Kassabova*	199
Tryst — *Sue Wootton*	200
She and Her First Best Boyfriend — *Dinah Hawken*	201
Makara — *Joan Fleming*	202
Cherries — *Renee Liang*	204
Newborn — *Emma Neale*	206
On a Son Returned to New Zealand — *Fleur Adcock*	208
August — *Stephanie Johnson*	209
Silly — *Meg Campbell*	211
6 The Eternal Sunshine of the Spotless Mind from Nine Movies — *Helen Rickerby*	212
I Love Those Photos — *Vivienne Plumb*	213
The Messenger — *Joanna Preston*	214
jill — *Brian Potiki*	216

dear heart — *Michele Leggott*	217
from The Time of the Giants — *Anne Kennedy*	220
Let's be honest here — *J C Sturm*	222
For Thee — *Hone Tuwhare*	223
Catch — *Murray Edmond*	224
Acknowledgements	227
Poet and artist biographies	236
About the editor	266
Index of titles and poets	267

Introduction

Love — that complicated, delicious, pleasurable, necessary feeling — ties us to another human, to a mother, father, son, daughter, sibling, lover or friend. Love can also tie us to a place, an experience, an object. We love and we are loved; unexpectedly, gloriously, painfully, deeply.

On the Going West Festival's final steam-train journey in 2005, Meg and Alistair Te Ariki Campbell read at the little chapel at Waikumete Cemetery. At one point they faced each other with such a look of love — enduring, strong, tender — the hairs on the back of my arms stood on end. I felt like I was trespassing, and then I heard the look of love translated within the lines of their poems.

This is what poetry can do. A poem can deliver a look of love that gives us goose bumps. Yet as this collection of love poems by New Zealand poets clearly shows, the poetic look of love takes many guises.

Love belongs in the real world not as some neo-platonic ideal that places a pure and untarnished love upon a pedestal, but as a feeling that includes grief along with joy, anger along with tenderness, frustration along with attentiveness.

Love poetry reflects this stretch of feeling.

The majority of the poems I have selected reveal adult love — from the sparks of youth to the changing nature of love in old age — but I have also included examples of the love of offspring (Janet Charman's 'warm loaf'), of particular places (Brian Turner's 'Remembering Summer') and of beloved objects (James Brown's 'The Bicycle'). Sometimes the poem is surprising as in Kate Camp's response to a black swan that supposedly fell in love with a plastic pedal boat shaped like a white swan ('Mute song'). At other times love is threaded into an extended narrative poem as in Anne Kennedy's *The Time of the Giants* and John Puhiatau Pule's *The Bond Of Time*. Some poets follow the tradition of using a particular form to frame aspects of love as in Andrew Johnston's sestina ('The Sounds') and Michele Leggott's sonnets in *dia*.

Poets have addressed the subject of love for centuries and, after all this time, it still remains a vital topic. Time-honoured motifs, such as the heart, the moon, flowers and the oceans, appear fresh in the service of love like an old grape that produces a new and delightful aftertaste. I have included a range of poems from the 1930s to the present day to highlight the shifting musical tones, vocabulary, motifs and attitudes across the decades, and while we may have to approach earlier poems with a different ear, these are poems that tap into universal constants and stand the test of time.

I have arranged the poems as though I were composing a symphony rather than sticking to a chronological rule, because I wanted poetic music along with poetic heart. Now it is over to the reader to explore the different echoes, the unexpected juxtapositions, the contours of tone, the historical links and disconnections, and the contemporary exposures.

Love has its origins in the intimacy of private lives, yet the poet makes 'the look of love' public to greater and to lesser degrees. While we should be cautious about trusting the truthfulness of poetry as autobiography, I have placed my trust in these poems to reveal diverse truths of love itself.

The anthology's title, *Dear Heart*, is borrowed from Michele Leggott's poem, which in turn borrowed it from the popular song by Henry Mancini (it also makes its way into Te Ariki Campbell's *Cages For the Wind*). Songs get under your skin; they make your body sway and your heart beat a little faster. With this anthology of heart poems, poems that may make you laugh, grimace, weep and feel *simpatico*, I invite you to trespass on the look of love; to move and to sway, to be moved and to be swayed.

— *Paula Green*

The Poems

Dream

— *Brian Turner*

If you were beside me now, the fire
cackling like my grandmother used to,
the sky soaked in stars, there's
a whole bucket of words and phrases
I would sing: garden, bloom, memories,
river, sky, tenderness, valley, tulip,
japonica, rose, your fair skin, breath,
happy smile, Stingo, varoom, sweetie darling,
a love of art and style and a hunger
for a fairy tale world without end.

Arohanui

— *Robert Sullivan*

Big love, that's what it means.
Aroha Nunui means huge love.
Aroha Nunui Rawa means very huge love.
Aroha Nunui Rawa Ake means bigger very huge love.
Aroha Nunui Rawa Ake Tonu
     means bigger enduring very huge love.
Aroha Nunui Rawa Ake Tonu Atu
     means biggest enduring hugest love,
which are some of the lengths and times of our longing

Love in the Early Winter

— *Jenny Powell*

I open the window
and breathe in so much air
that the rest of the world pauses
through lack of oxygen.
I am gulping in the serenity
of early winter in the morning.
There's no bustle of breeze
so the grasses are still,
and the water race is duty bound
to reflect a frame of land.
This is the best season for light,
which flings itself
in acrobatic angles on whatever
takes its fancy.

The view spreads
up the valley and waits
by the hills.

Wedding song

— *Jenny Bornholdt*

Now you are married
try to love the world
as much as you love
each other. Greet it as your husband,
wife. Love it with all your
might as you sleep
breathing against its back.

Love the world, when, late at night,
you come home to find snails
stuck to the side of the house
like decoration.

Love your neighbours.
The red berries on their trampoline
their green wheelbarrow.

Love the man walking on
water, the man up a
mast. Love the light moving
across the *Island Princess*.

Love your grandmother when she tells you
her hair is three-quarters 'cafe au lait'.

Try to love the world, even when you discover
there is no such thing as   *The Author*
any more.

Love the world, praise
god, even, when your aerobics instructor
is silent.

Try very hard to love
your mailman, even though he regularly
delivers you Benedicto Clemente's mail.

Love the weta you find on the path,
injured by alteration.

Love the tired men, the burnt
house, the handlebars of light
on the ceiling.

Love the man on the bus who says
it all amounts to a fishing rod
or a light bulb.

Love the world of the garden.
The keyhole of bright green grass
where the stubborn palm
used to be,
bees so drunk on ginger flowers
that they think the hose water
is rain   your hair tangled in
heartsease.   Love the way,
when you come inside,
insects find their way out
from the temporary rooms of
your clothes.

The Apple Picker

— *Sarah Jane Barnett*

We walk out to the orchard.
You speak of an apple's slow shift
from mottled green to red,
pick one off the ground,
roll the indecisive skin in your hands.

Pickers move slowly between trees
cradling woven baskets.
Dogs chase geese that rise
from the grass like flung arms.

Back against bark, you cut a *Pink Lady*
so the pips form a star,
hollow out the core, dig the knife tip
under each seed, and with a practised motion,
remove the skin in a single ribbon.
The scent of apple spreads
sweet and tart between us.

Love poem

— *Gregory O'Brien*

Houses are likened to shoeboxes but shoeboxes are not likened to houses. A car is likened to a heap but a heap is not likened to a car. A child is a terror but terror is not a child. A business might be a sinking ship but a sinking ship is no business. A bedroom is a dog's breakfast but a dog's breakfast is not a bedroom. A bad review might be a raspberry but a raspberry is not a bad review. A haircut is likened to a disaster but a disaster is not a haircut. Books can be turkeys but turkeys are never books. A holiday might be a riot but a riot is not a holiday. A garden might become a headache but a headache is not a garden. I dream about you but you are not a dream.

Apartment

— *Virginia Were*

You held my skull in your big
hands as if everything in it
was precious.
Coins of blue and yellow light
flew across the ceiling.
Like the cover of *Goat's Head
Soup*, you said when I pointed
them out.

I remember the way the curtains
swelled with the breeze, your hands
passing through my hair,
over my brow, until I no longer
knew which was my arm, your hand,
my belly, your chest.
Your smooth skin might as well
have been my own as we skimmed
the quickening shadows
of your room.

Son

— *Angela Andrews*

He fingers the tendon
that runs along your arm
as you read to him.
He's needling into a small space.
There's a pulse down there,
close to the surface
at that particular point
in the wrist, and a nerve
tunnelling out
to finger-test weather —
sensory endings in skin.

Love Poem for a Love a Long Time Ago

— *Airini Beautrais*

This was in the days of Jane Austen
and floral pyjamas. In the days of
'far across a sea of . . .'
Ladies, only think:
the man with a strange haircut
in the half-lit hallway
could have been the boy
you picked daisies over.

Audrey

— *Charles Spear*

You fly a kite against a silver sky;
Your tranquil loveliness, pale by the wane
Of sighing tides, gleams like a butterfly
White-crystal-winged in slanting straws of rain.

[but you . . .]
— *Wystan Curnow*

                                          but you
                                          love I
                                          knew by
                                          heart

Love Poem for the Tauherenikau River

— *Airini Beautrais*

I don't know where you start
or even end.
I have only been to your middle.
It is always me and one other.
Along your banks we eat kawakawa berries
mouthfuls of grit and pepper.
We slide naked into the same sun-filled hole
our splashes blur the clearness of your water.
We move stones and you move them back
and move them on again; the hushed current
follows its course.

The Verb to Give
— *Dinah Hawken*

for Al and Kate

If you count *give away* as in marriage,
one to the other, and *give onto*
as a room gives onto a brilliant city,
and if you count *give out* as in the dawn
-till-dusk-till-dawn of love, and *give in*
as kowhai leaves give in to wind, and if you count
give off as in giving off allure, the vibrato
of the body, and *give over* as this day
is given over to the pleasures of a wedding,
and if you count *give up* as we give ourselves
up like gulls to friends and wind and children,

the verb to give has thirty-six senses
(twice as many as the verb to love)
and so thrives on being received.

ASK ME HOW
I WOULD DESCRIBE
this whole
BEAUTIFUL
THING WELL IF
I WERE A BELL
I'D GO DING DONG DING
DONG DING

The Beach House

— James K Baxter

The wind outside this beach house
Shaking the verandah rail
Has the weight of the sky behind its blows,
A violence stronger than the fable

Of life and art. Sitting alone
Late at the plywood table,
I have become a salt-scoured bone
Tumbling in the drifted rubble,

And you, my love, sleep under quilts within
The square bunk-room. When I was young
(Hot words and brandy on my tongue)
Only the grip of breast, mouth, loin,

Could ward off the incubus
Of night's rage. Now I let
The waters grind me, knowing well that the sweet
Daybreak behind your eyes

Will not be struck dead by any wind,
And we will walk on the shore
A day older, while the yoked waves thunder,
As if the storm were a dream. Sleep sound.

talk about a tonic

— *Diane Brown*

last night at dinner a famous poet
proclaimed I was so suddenly
beautiful, someone somewhere

must love me — of course he's prone
to lyricism and I'm not sure
if he's confused like most men

between lust and love,
but whatever the feeling
it works like photosynthesis

the heat of your thoughts
even at this distance settling
a faint brush of colour on my cheeks

Glenburn

— *Paula Green*

Even in the face of an icy wind, the stillness
dazzles us, and we journey south to the dulcet honey.
He falls silent, the din left destitute, far
from the hive. The sound of his laugh, it rises
and becomes music, a vein of sun that is in him

like a mountain. Appearances remain objects of barter.
All that calm. All that fury. We cross a threshold
to witness the unbidden cloud. Our chamber of words
sweetened as if made of honey or beeswax,
for we arrive at last, the smell now in him of hive.

We will eat bread and cheese, forgetting the northern
city, the pull of the ocean. He moves with his sight
fixed on stillness, finding a fickle appearance
like a star behind slow speech. All that fury. All that calm.
Where will we find the scale of love? The journey south

undoes the mountain of cloud, his own incubus
the riddle that is land. We are certain that buildings
will appear in the stillness, kept alive by our eyes.

Wild Daisies

— *Bub Bridger*

If you love me
Bring me flowers
Wild daisies
Clutched in your fist
Like a torch
No orchids or roses
Or carnations
No florist's bow
Just daisies
Steal them
Risk your life for them
Up the sharp hills
In the teeth of the wind
If you love me
Bring me daisies
Wild daisies
That I will cram
In a bright vase
And marvel at

wedding song

— *Bernadette Hall*

a duck in a gum tree
    a lamb on a swing
and is this not the strangest thing,
    to dance wifely, husbandly to sing

*

the old Lagonda tearooms
    blue lagoon ice-cream
seeds shaken in a silver sieve
    waxed paper in the cake tin

*

beside the lake of greeny-blue
    beside the lake of bluey-green
this surely is a wondrous thing
    to dance husbandly, wifely to sing

Ruby's heirloom dress

— *Elizabeth Smither*

Great-great-grandmother pulled on her thimble
and pricked her needle through the smocking
the yoke made a tiny silk plain above it
below flowed the skirt with embroidered rosebuds.

Great-great-grandmother's long fingers and bent skull
are gone from the world but tenderness is left
in the fall of the skirt, the complex lines of smocking
the little apertures the cream and pink thread makes

like tiny windows, since you are tiny,
open like casements over your heart.
Everything in your dress is openness: the neck
delicately trimmed with lace, the sleeves gathered in

with ribbon and rosebuds, the floating hem as if
great-great-grandmother was sailing around the world
stopping at islands with fruit and palm trees
and a soft sea with waves the way the hem falls.

The castle

— *Fiona Farrell*

Three knights rode up to the castle wall
and one brought her roses. A dozen,
crimson, their buds tightly furled, their
prickles removed and bound up in gold
ribbon. These flowers, he said, were a
symbol of love. They would last, like his
love, forever. She put them in a vase on
the table where they stood upright,
declaiming devotion. The second knight
came riding, head bare to the sky, and
brought her flowers from the roadside:
buttercups for the sunshine at her white
throat, kanuka for a new manner of
speaking, wild roses whose prickles
tore at her skin. "Here you are," he said.
"These won't last the day — but they're
pretty, eh?" She put them in a jamjar on
the windowsill. Their petals peeled away
like silk petticoats. They fell to the floor,
crumpled on polished wood. The third
knight came to her with empty hands, but
clear eyes. The castle was old. Its rooms
were cold. "You don't need flowers," he
said. "What you need is wood for your
fire." The next day he brought her one
dozen dry logs. The room became pink
and warm as a beating heart. Her
petticoats fell away from her like petals

to polished wood and she stepped from
them like a lily bud. He gathered her
then and they rode away from the castle,

through the wide fields,

singing.

keeping warm

— *Michele Leggott*

you there at
the long end
of my arm

drive me to
work & back
over the bridge

to distraction
icecreams in
the wind or

moon on the
beach : *them
dauphins*

berserk about
us on their
offshore roads

razzle dazzle
moonlight
climb up the

near side of
heaven's cloudy
smile : this is

heaven & you
in it following
la vie dansante

warm rowdy
voice reading
to the kids

draped word
perfect about
you doing

equal parts
charm & need
for me looking

on decoding
nuance (oh
clouds) the house

needs a paint
the Saturday
skilsaws howl

into September
& cups of tea
punctuate the

hard questions
: there was a
moment when

that look in
your eye closed
all distances

ka-boom as
the poets say
dreamily

two people
get together
like *spring*

and *moon*
time & place
fold around

them : yes
there's specific
moonlight and

a curve in
the road where
it takes your

breath away
this is local
right here up

close & it's
your bridge to
where I stand

laughing at
it already
written in

big glittering
letters : let's
go out there

and do the poem

Love Song

— *Rachel McAlpine*

your forehead
is the curve
of the world

through your eyes
I slide
into a jungle
a tangle
of flying vines
of blood feasts
of jagged cries
of silent
silken
steps

your blood
has the beat
of the sea
it pulls
to the pulse
of the moon

if I die
before I lie
with you
rocks will rain
from heaven
on my grave

Brightness

— *Denis Glover*

I am bright with the wonder of you
And the faint perfume of your hair

I am bright with the wonder of you
You being far away or near

I am bright with the wonder of you
Warmed by your eyes' blue fire

I am bright with the wonder of you
And your mind's open store

I am bright with the wonder of you
Despite the dark waiting I endure

I am bright with the wonder of you.

Inesilla

— *Bill Manhire*

I am here, Inesilla,
gazing up at your window.
All of Seville
is darkness and sleep.

I am here with my cloak,
with my guitar and sword,
with what makes me bold.
I am here at your window.

Do you sleep, Inesilla? Well
I will soon wake you with song,
and if the old fellow stirs
there's always this blade.

Ah let fall from the sill
that handhold of silk.
Why are you so slow?
Can it mean there's a rival?

I am here, Inesilla.
I am here at your window.
All of Seville
is darkness and sleep.

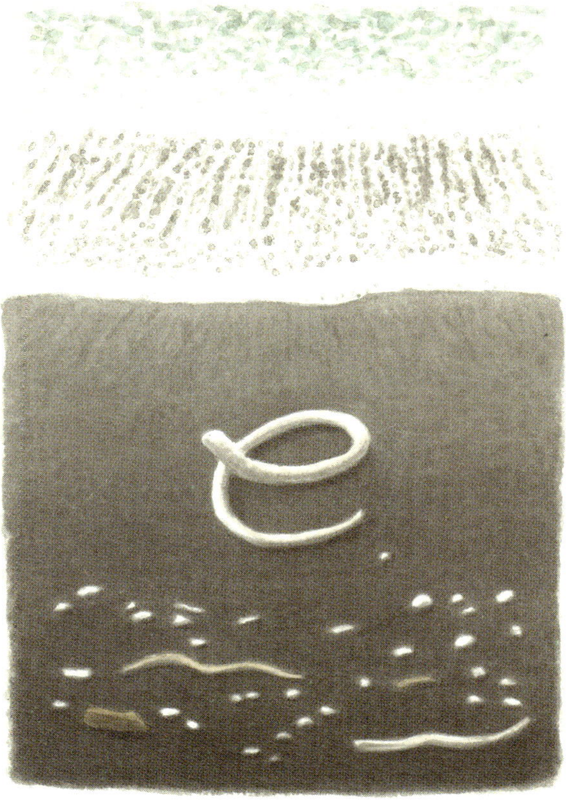

Billet-doux

— *Michael Harlow*

And a candle
too, all its fires
flying quietly
wingtips of light
for you as bright
this astonishment
of a lemon-coloured
sun I send over
the hill, may they
your heart hold
still, and full this
plainsong love
to sing this day,
and all years be
my pretty pleasured
by as much laughter
as we can bear.

Love by Candlelight

— *Mary Stanley*

Lift up your brown arms
   And let fall your heavy hair.
Here no one may enter
None climb this stair.

Bend down your ripe mouth.
   Love's fire-bright silence, this
Half-painful, shadow haunted
So-much-longed-for kiss.

Open your green eyes.
   Pin-points of candleshine
In caverns of coolness gleam
Here, close to mine.

Rest your dear head night-long
   In its accustomed place.
I seek no other heav'n
Beyond your mortal face.

To Utopias

— *Ian Wedde*

They always fade away, these nowheres,
There are streetlights in paradise, 'our golden children dance
On broken glass', dark, gothic and revived
The mitred peaks pierce the clouds and time
'Stands still'. Hamilton's jetboat is our brush

Now, painting its frothing wake through gorges
Bituminous, dark, and kind of Dutch. I want
To meet you for lunch and to eat rice noodles
In a broth with clams, prawns, and chopped scallions.
I want to watch you eating while I talk

And then I want to drink my soup while you
Impersonate the garrulous media types who chew
Your ear. I want to chew your ear at lunch-
Time while time stands still and broth
Froths around piquant peaks of cloud-piercing

Dreams. And then I want to walk with you
Through a golden city whose spires aspire to heaven
And beneath whose pavings rivers run down
To ripraps at the harbour's edge and those beaches of broken
Shining glass shards where children dance.

We dream. When you dream your body bucks
Like a jetboat in the bed, your hair gets wet,
And when you wake you have that nowhere look
Of someone who doesn't know what time it is
In this bituminous gorge of backlit peaks.

Tipple Over Tail

— *Johanna Emeney*

Today,
when you raised
that ghost of a phrase

from somewhere deep
in the Yorkshire Dales,
I fell for you all over again.

Head over heels.

You

— *C K Stead*

Our friends' wedding:
I'd lied, called it a funeral
to get army leave
so I could be with you.
It was a surprise, a present
and your blush of pleasure
cheered me like a crowd.

So here we are on the step
above the 'happy couple'
who will one day divorce —
looking into the future
which is now.

Ten friends together
in that photograph.
Fifty years on
and four are dead.
Who will be next?
Who will be last
and put out the light?

It's time to tell you again
how much I loved the girl
who blushed her welcome.
Forgive my trespasses.
Stay close. Hold my hand.

grahams beach, bach

— *Sonja Yelich*

this kiss we take
is made for our hips
we salmon on in to each other's clocks
with a light switch on string
you pull from the ceiling

*

& here we are arriving
at the sugar of our lives

*

our children sleeping in their
weeny duvet skins —
kina & creamery

*

what price would you pay
& from which shop

*

the sea out front
is a font in italic —
the forward curl

*

we think how lucky we are
on the peninsula.

The Miracle

— *Jack Ross*

The four tuis in the tree
are back   clearly something
there they like   yellow
bell-shaped flowers

Bronwyn's cooking toffee
squares in the next
room   sun angling
down the hill

Are you mid-thought?
she asks me   signs & omens
Mairangi on a bus   3 x 13
the boombox sings

The miracle is you & me

Bear Dance

— Peter Bland

for Beryl

To bring you to my bed
I must dramatise myself:
I must walk through the house
in primary colours.

How else can I be seen
among all the children and flowers
among all the music and mirrors
among all the open windows
that surround us?

I have to shout
to wear bright shirts
to dance up and down
rattling the cups in the kitchen.

The children laugh.
They say I'm a bear.
They like it best when I roll on the ground.
They say there's a dancing bear in the house.

But this is my love dance.
Aheee . . . I bellow . . .
clicking my throat like the starlings
in the early morning
when they think they've swallowed the sun.

This, I say, is my love dance.
Later I shall paint your image.
There'll be a bold but awkward tenderness
trembling in each line . . .
I'll be struggling to overcome my clumsiness
with the strength of my love.

These are my charms —
my bear dance and my image of you.
With these I'll bring you to my bed
again and again.

When you see me in my bright shirt
when you hear neighbours and friends complaining
saying I'm loud and heavy-footed
remember that my dance is for you.
It's in your sole honour.
It has to compete with your silence
and with the other silences that go on and on
like the sky through this open window
for ever . . .

For the father of my children
— *Karlo Mila*

It would take more than a
sharp shock
to unravel us

more than
what might catch the corner
of a cardigan
or fray fabric

parts of me are stitched inside your hem
your name sewn on
the bottom of my feet

even a sly glance
misplaced kiss
foul rumour

could not

interlocked
we are
not just
limbs, tongues, lips

all the cells we have to offer the world
are intertwined into something more certain
than the sum
of our own thin threads

together we have walked the line
of descent

The Wish

— *Kevin Ireland*

She asked me what
I might desire:
her flesh, her mind,
her eyes of fire?

I asked one wish
and one alone:
a kiss, a leaf,
a river stone.

From these I'll build
a wall that's vast,
a roof above
and love that lasts.

Husband to Wife

— *Chris Tse*

With the road tied
into your hair

and your tongue
bent to speak only
       true words
you will find your way back to Guangzhou.

It's a haze there in the room
where you keep my photo,

windows boarded up
the outside world erased,
a thousand hearts beat
out of time in your mouth.

O sweet one — what has become
       of you?

Now you are
no wilder
nor more dangerous
than that stifled song in your throat.

Come, I want to treat you
rice wine and dim sums.

Great Full Moon, Lowering Behind the Black Hill

— Anna Livesey

The lucky mouth
tastes of strawberries.

*

If searched long enough,
the fruit is found,
hanging or destroyed,
rising or lowering
into the black hills.

*

Softness. Do we love it?
Do we take the long strands
and worship them?
Does it lift us? Do we rise more easily, or is it
like the green vine on the bare peach —
winding, low intent, creeping?

Poem for Kereihi

— *Hone Tuwhare*

My love is really iron
    when she cries
    and softer than
    a pound of butter
    when she kisses me.

My love is a painter.
    My love looks at things just
    like a camera . . . clicking: also.

My love feeds the cat
    and the dog, her children
    and sometimes me — when
    I need a place to catch
    my breath & to watch the stars break out at night.

My love consults the silence of
    the trees; the wind trickling
    sand through its fingers; listening
    to wave-talk that is really a clamour
    of many tongues insisting that although
    things may get worser than worse, it
    will be better next time! My love is iron.

At the Beginning of Love

— *Elizabeth Smither*

You could put on a winter coat
walk up the wide steps of a gallery
past pillars and porticoes
into the room with Seurats

stand in front of one gazing
almost ready to weep at
except outbursts are forbidden
how solid the shimmering bodies

how like dense marble the water
and the grass: rapiers
the clouds: zeppelins, the gazing
eyes, satisfied and smug philosophers.

Child

— *Janet Frame*

When I was a child I wore a fine tartan coat
that my grandmother, woman of might,
magnificent launcher of love and old clothes, had set afloat
on a heaving relative sea
of aunt and cousin and big enfolding wave of mother
down to small wave of me.

Oh happily I stood that day in the school playground
near the damp stone wall
and the perilous nine o'clock wind
grabbed at my coat-sleeve, waving it in a bright wand
of yellow and green and blue
— all colours, and the other children loved me
and the little girls pleaded to lend
their skipping-rope and the boys their football.

But the spell soon broke in my hand.
Love and sleeve together fell.
The wind blew
more perilous when the world found
my tartan coat was not even *new*.

a

Words and Roses

— *Alistair Te Ariki Campbell*

from Cages For the Wind
for my dear Meg, with love

I never imagined so rare a night
would make me dream of roses —
the gentle rain,
the words falling irresistibly
as arrows in flight,
sometimes singly,
sometimes in a shower,
far too many for me to catch,
and each a flower
without match.

In what other life did you wear them
so that they smelt of you?
We knew each other well,
these words and I,
from having sung of you everywhere
under your spell.

I followed them to the source
somewhere north of your heart —
or was it more to the south?
It matters only that they came,
from whichever direction,
still warm from your mouth.

Dear heart, I had forgotten everything
I learnt that love disposes,
until last night they came again
in a dream
with the gentle rain,
smelling of you and roses.

Christmas Day, 1998

If She Hadn't Been There

— *Brian Turner*

For Tulip

A man sat down to write a love poem
    and thought of clouds like rent fabric
as if falcons had ripped a dreamcoat to bits
    and spread the pieces all over the sky.

Beautiful he thought, and lovely the way
    cool water rushes green and silver
over greywacke and schist
  prised from the mountains before his time.

Today, he thought, the light in her eyes
    shines like sunshine on mayflies' wings.
And today, because he is a New Zealander,
  he thinks of scarlet and green, of rata

and keas, of pukekos and their pervy-princeliness,
    of yellowhammers and godwits,
of the *kee-aa* cries that are just as thrilling
  as the sound of nightingales singing

in Berkeley Square. He thinks of down
    and sheen and kindness and care.
He thinks of what he would be now
  if she hadn't been there.

A Late Honeymoon

— *Iain Lonie*

We are wearing exactly the clothes
for such summer expeditions —
practical, worn to dullness, confining:
the hats against the sun, the laced boots for walking,
our broadcloth statements about Nature.

Standing here, a little separate
the rough ground of rocks and bushes between
we see the sea's blueness framed
by two grotesque pinnacles,
chalk at this distance glinting like ice

but ready to crumble obediently
under the master touch of winter rains.
Returning, we shall draw closer
on the downward path to the hotel
where white curtains billow by an open window.

We do not speak at all
feeling no need for conversation:
the afternoon holds us in its golden arms.
Tonight I shall write in my diary:
'Walked to clifftop with H. Fine view of sea.'

Such fantastic shapes the rain carves!
But you can't beat the sea for simplicity
and the statements of flat calm.
Look: far out, a breeze has caught two tiny sails
and draws them steadily to the white horizon.

The ngaio tree

— *Fiona Kidman*

we leave best what we have truly loved
— LAURIS EDMOND

So here come the kids, skidding their school bags
across the floor, blazers flung awry on the chairs,
                          two grandsons
of which there are five brothers in all.
'We've had exams today,' they say, exasperated,
'And we had to do that poem, the one you wrote
about Dad's tree house in the ngaio. We knew
we'd get it sooner or later. Toby said so,
                          and Reuben too.'
'So what did they ask you?'
'Oh you know, stuff about what does the poem *mean*?'
                          'And you said?'
I'm focusing on the hot chocolate now,
            pouring it into two mugs.

'That our dad had a tree house and you used to yell
at him to come down when it got dark and raining.'
'Nothing about bad dreams and conquering fear?'
                          One of them sighs.
'Teachers don't know our dad. Our dad's our dad.'
That's true enough, more that than my son any more
and besides, the *meaning* of the wretched poem
has shifted.   The red-headed woodsman
shakes his head regularly over the fragile

branches, the thin screen of foliage,
the tree's increasing vulnerability
as another gale sweeps in scattering dry twigs
                                      ribbons in the sky.
'Don't know how much more it can take,' he says,
                       laconic, commiserating.

But there are some things I do know:
if we stand on the lawn beneath that tree
we see far beyond us dark fires of sunsets
settling over the bay, pastel new moons
cavorting across the sky, the delphinium
days of summer, mists resting in the far
hills like the foothills of the Himalayas
and yes the dark scribble of the tree's branches
against stormy skies, even though the boy came down
                              from the tree long ago,

there is all this and more. At some time
or another, every person I have truly loved,
our close family circle, the aunts
            (save Roberta who never made it here),
the old old companions of my childhood,
                               all the true friends
have stood beneath this tree.
                And I tell myself
that, so long as I live, if the roots hold
fast to the bank below and new green shoots
appear on the branches each spring, all will be
                              as well as it can.

Puriri

— *Jan Kemp*

A puriri moth's wing
lies light in my hand —

my breath can lift it
light as this torn wing

we lie on love's breath.

Before I Get into Sleep with You

— Janet Frame

Before I get into sleep with you
I want to have been
into wakefulness, too.

Embrace

— Robin Hyde

A bee zooms, deep amid the warm young grasses.
Startled, the rose
Laughs, and sways backward from the wind, her lover . . .
'Fool . . . he will see . . .'
But that brown thief, grown bolder,
Unclasps the brooch of dew upon her shoulder
And draws her very close
That he may see her white breast rise and fall . . .
Now, she cares not what passes —
Shadow, or leaf, or bee —
She does not care at all.

A white star shines, a branch of almond glistens . . .
They hear . . . they see . . .
Loosen your arms about me, in this quiet
Of dusk, this lonely room
Where ghosts of amber roses haunt the gloom.
You do not heed . . . and a slow moment passes,
Hushed as the wind among the blue-black grasses,
Deep as an indrawn breath —
Ah, so your love stay nigh me
I care not what goes by me,
Splendour, or youth, or death —
I care not what star listens,
What silvered almond tree.

Life eternal

— *Diana Bridge*

the silver of

his whistling
her singing

from the kitchen
Schubert's *Impromptu*

though neither
knew it

life eternal
good as

Time of Day

— *Hinemoana Baker*

All the clocks in the house
show slightly different times.
How did this happen?

I must be responsible.
I stretch in the moving sun
one paw in the light.

You haven't had a drink
for eighteen months.
Last night you said

*I want us to be old ladies
together.* I lit the fire,
we listened to the dark

sea outside pounding
the foundations.
In an hour you'll roar up

the drive and break
the seal of the door,
you'll rinse a clanging

teapot, you'll smell of coffee,
you'll tell me to *guess
what guess what honey* —

His eyes

— *Joanna Margaret Paul*

he
held onto me with
his eyes

until
trembling an idea
arose

like
a small boy on the
brink

or
him having the ball
&

I
there with my arms
open

I love peaches

— *Vivienne Plumb*

I like eating peaches in my hand on the back doorstep,
and our long southern summer nights
with the cobalt sky splashed with stars.
I like planning pleasures for the future,
and swimming. I like that.
And love I like, but I prefer to talk about peaches.
I can understand them, skin to stone
and then you eat them.
But love: untried, untasted,
a peach still too firm, too fuzzy,
overripe, or sour and undergrown.

Traveller overdue

— *Emma Neale*

A sound like an animal's hiss
along the chimney's thin, dark marrow
to the still blood-warm grate.
A flurry of flakes at the window.
A powdering of snow on the driveway cobbles.
White trees protrude bony wrists on the air.
A single night bird turns in the stillness,
cry like a rock that cracks a frozen lake.

The house's heartbeat has dropped
to a metre like the measure of your footfall in the alps:
slow, deep, each outline pressed more heavily
by the weight of your pack:
shovel,

       harness,

              food,

                       ropes,

                             axe.

Against the polar moonlight
I try to believe the toe of each boot
is defined and steady as a pen's stylus,
and the trails your steps cut
against a paper the winter mills and mills
are the lines of a letter you're writing home to us
which details the deliriously, miraculously usual:
I'm here, fine, on my way. Soon.

lovesong

— *Bernadette Hall*

for JR

missing you
like I've been hit
and missing you
for years

in a doorway
somewhere between
the kitchen
and the laundry

missing the way
you tell me every day
I'm beautiful

putting a kiss
on my forehead
when I'm sick

and on my tongue
a sweet exotic tincture
with your tongue

we could call it
ha-ka-ta-ra-me-a

because

— *Sarah Broom*

it was because he loved her so much
that the clock got smashed and the wings fell
off the day, because he loved her so much
that all the maps flew up into the sky
and burnt up along the edges of the sun,
because he loved, yes, because, that the teapot
started talking about longing and the spoons
were screaming themselves hoarse, something
about the way they had to wait, it was because
that he loved her, the way the airport sang
its greasy songs right inside his ear again
and again, because it was he loved it was
so much that the room started raining all over,
warm and tropical, the kind of water you
can breathe, because it was her so much
it was he loved, the way the clock just kept on
ticking through the broken night and the windows
had to hold themselves so tight just to stay
like they were supposed to be, upright,
rectangular, transparent to the world because
it was so much you see it was so much

My Mother's Voice

— *Ingrid Horrocks*

December 2007

My mother's voice
crackled and deepened
on the tape recorder.

She spoke to me only
yesterday, but already the effort
to speak across such great

distance,
from her twenties
to me in my thirties,

stretched the tape,
like the whirr of
static ghosts.

Transcribing her disembodied
words how I want
her here to hold
my body to her breast.

White Gold

— *Jenny Powell*

I wear the wedding ring
of my own mother and her
sometimes mother; two
generations of gold melted
moulded and smothered
in a layer of silver
marked in marcasite, white
gold my mother calls it.

This is the ring of weddings
in name, swift ceremonies
and the change from Miss to Mrs;
this is the ring of weddings
where bride after bride is mother
to a child of the heart, desired
with a burning fit to kill.

I wear the wedding ring
of my sometimes mother
and her own mother as if
it was made for my finger.
I am marked by marcasite,
smothered in silver and branded
by the white heat of their gold.

Fontanello

— Anna Jackson

Now you have closed your fontanelle,
my son, my fontanello, I only know

you through the words that serve
thought with sound and saliva

away from the peachy smell
that never meant anything to me

but presence. Your presence,
little present, fontanello, at my skin.

Oh fontanello, let me in.
Your words are little chinks

through to you, and little bricks
that wall me out. Whisper and shout,

you'll go further than this, I'm reeling you out,
and letting you in, always, fontanello,

ready, once more, to begin.
Look at you, so tall and thin.

Still Life

— *Joanna Margaret Paul*

You rocked the cradle
I wrote & read
& searched an image for our childs eye
(leaf petal pool tadpole)
& said
this likening
is loving merely
& when you came to bed
the two wine glasses overlapped
the white pot plant drew close to the camellia
& one green curtain embraced the whole.

A Lightning Tree

— *Cilla McQueen*

my wild love seeks a fastening place
but passion kills with heaviness
I want to give you tenderness
not deadly electricity

so I have made of words a lightning tree
to earth my dangerous love through poetry.

r

The nervous public speaker

— *Lauris Edmond*

There it was, the red jacket —
it lit up the distance
with the dark gleam
Black Doris plums have
before they ripen,
or a crimson hibiscus.

Among suited shoulders
earth-black, she carried it
like a flower, a flame,
cell of light in the careful
dimness audiences create.
Perched on my risky rock

I kept looking up, watching
for that bright centre
— the door that opens to
a first chink of morning
in a windowless hut,
the safety of sun.

Falter or freeze as I might,
this shimmer of love
remained: my daughter,
with me this side of the dark,
nest of joy perched
on a trembling branch.

Puer Natus

— Mary Stanley

My little son, lie down to sleep
clothed in your tender warmth, by love
wrapped round to cheat the wintry night
brilliant with stars and frost beyond the wall.
A belly filled with milk is feast
enough, no Barmecide may hang
your hunger on an empty plate.
Such comfort's in a thumb the rich
might envy, and no palace holds
an infant king more crowned than this
whose curls I cover with my kiss.

The Sounds

— *Andrew Johnston*

Rain, a restful place: a plain
negotiation led to this, one small
lit room, in lieu of a camera, and the
drowned valleys, windless, listening
to the rain, on leaf, on water
in winter. Disentangled thus, we touch

as if deciphering a prophecy, we touch
as ocean, held by the land, made plain
a difficult map, whose cove-smooth water
uncoils with travel, surrounds a small
arrival, a larger departure. Listening
to the sounds as we pronounce them, the

waves, the bright particulars, we hear the
way we've been so far, we touch
speech, our bodies fearless listening
devices. And days unravel as on a plain
a road will travel straight with small
perceptible corrections. But water

under the hand of the wind, and water
in darkness: things we see and cannot tell, the
sounds are full of these too, as small
fish, late, in a bell of light, touch
the surface once and disappear. It's plain
each morning, talking and not listening,

how plain things aren't, how whether we're listening
or not, the sounds go on around us, and water
will erase all previous arrangements. It's plain
how prophecies succumb before the
evidence, words in sand that crumble at a touch,
that need to be unwritten or forgotten, and small

reliable ambitions fashioned, parts for a small
cast — two, who move from stage to stage, listening
to the places where their different futures touch.
Rain-fast, a stream falls, to clear salt water
where just such a lean crew rows, the
dinghy iffing and butting, a plain

afternoon. The small boat drums the mingling water;
the rowers, listening, will remember the
sounds, when they touch, that these days made plain.

A Letter

— *David Mitchell*

I am here my love
beneath an apricot sky.

Summer is a young girl,
her voice is thick

in these green islands.

The valley gorse was burning
last week. Quietly in the night.

Tonight it is warm. Just a song bird
and the hills.

It is not lonely, but very slow.

I am here my love.
This is all

my beauty.

Quarantine Island

— *Harry Ricketts*

for Helen and Marc on their wedding

Love is and is not the point.
With this high wind filling your sails,
world turns strange and yet the same.

Your craft must be delicate, also tough.
You head for open, unplumbed seas.
Love is and is not the point.

These charts you've packed are full of blanks,
bluffs and sounds you must rename.
World turns strange and yet the same.

Tempests, typhoons, the taniwha stowed away
in the hold: all can be weathered.
Love is and is not the point.

There will be days of sudden calm,
nights when stars burn into your head.
World turns strange and yet the same.

The unknown calls. The day is yours.
Hope and trust will take you far.
Love is and is not the point.
World turns strange and yet the same.

A new plateau song

— *Sam Hunt*

I have a son I love
as a father loves a son,
a woman I love
as a man loves a woman:

such love is huge
in its normality:
no one makes any
mention of the mountain

adrift above their town.
They know it's there
and don't need any
word of it from me.

I have a son I love
and there is fog on the
shoulder of the mountain
as a father loves a son.

The woman, same, she
comes from under the mountain.
I tell of my love for her
and the fog giving over.

A woman, boy and a man
walk down from the mountain:
such normality
needs no word from me:

except to say
the woman is the woman I love,
the boy, my son. I am the man.
And this is our mountain.

As big as a father

— *Jeffrey Paparoa Holman*

I lost him the first time
before I could grasp
who he was, what he did, where
he fitted with her

and it's always seemed so dumb:
how to lose something
as big as a father.

I lost him the next time
to the rum-running Navy
who took him and took him
and kept right on taking

and it wasn't my mistake
losing a vessel
as big as a father.

I lost him a third time
to a ship in a bottle
that rocked him and rocked him
and shook out his pockets

and no kind of magic
could slip me inside
with my father.

I lost him at home
when floorboards subsided
as he said and she said
went this way and that way

and dead in the water
I couldn't hang on
to my father.

The last time I lost him
I lost him for good:
the night and the day
the breath he was breathing

and death's head torpedoes
blew out of the water
the skiff of my father.

Inventing You

— *Kevin Ireland*

If I were to forget the way I think of you,
break you to bits, jumble you up
and sweep away all sign of you,

and then if I were to start all over again
and invent you, with nothing more
to work on than a notion of your waiting

to be discovered, I would not approach
the problem by trying to make you solid,
giving you shape, attaching so many yards

of pretended skin to so much meat and bone.
The museums are full of lively examples
of that kind of solution — yet when

the attendants are not looking, my touch
detects stone. Instead, I would take silence
and begin with one sound, then another,

to fill first the air and the seas and the bush,
then the towns, with your softness.
If I were to forget the way I think of you

and then invent you all over again,
I would assemble you from sigh and laughter,
from half-words and whispers,

from breathing in and breathing out,
from the rustle of love — even the rub
that skin makes, touching in sleep.

The Language of Bluff

— *Cilla McQueen*

The language of Bluff
is tender and blunt
when it comes to love.

Your fingers to my temple,
a soft, rough touch.

With your fisherman's knife
you slash a red bloom
from the rosebush, Erotica.

You read me cloud-currents,
tweak my ears to the westerly
rumbling storm-breakers
out beyond Auahi.

Your afterimage
inscribes the present;
your absence
a sort of sickening enchantment.

Husband and Wife Talk Without Talking at a Difficult Dinner Party

— *Joan Fleming*

Their elbows on the table are *yang*, their backs against the hip, uncomfortable chairs are *yang*, the jokes are witty and cruel, the bread-crust hard, the red wine sharp and showy. When she unhooks an earring and pulls at the lobe of her left ear, he knows she has a headache. When he starts shredding the paper napkin, she knows he is thinking about his father's jumpy, medicated heart. He drinks more, and she stops drinking. It is for the same reason. Her earring tings against an empty wine glass. His father, miles away, tosses in his sleep. Underneath the table, their bare feet find each other, *yin*, arch against arch, making a soft space where speech can grow, in the darkness.

After Apollinaire

— *Jack Ross*

	Il y a des petits ponts épatants
I	There's a big steel harbour bridge
	Il y a mon coeur qui bat pour toi
crush	There's my heart beating for you
	Il y a une femme triste sur la route
you	There's a woman trundling across the road
	Il y a un beau petit cottage dans un jardin
against	There's a fibrolite bach in a garden
	Il y a six soldats qui s'amusent comme des fous
my	There's six skateboarders crapping out like loons
	Il y a mes yeux qui cherchent ton image
breast	There's my eyes searching for you
like	There's a stand of eucalyptus trees on Forrest Hill
	(& an old campaigner who pisses as we pass)
the	There's a poet dreaming about his Chantal
	There's a beautiful Chantal in that big Auckland
dove	There's a pill-box on a cliff-top
	There's a farmer trucking his sheep
a	There's my life which belongs to you
	There's my black ballpoint scribbling scribbling
little	There's a screen of poplars intricate intricate
	There's my old life which is definitely *over*
girl	There's narrow streets near K Rd where we've loved each other
	There's a chick in Freemans Bay who drives her friends INSANE
strangles	There's my driver's licence in my wristbag

              There's Mercs and Beamers on the road
without
              There's love
noticing   There's life
              I adore you

from dia

— *Michele Leggott*

From the corner of this mouth take
kisses that begin in moonlight
and pitch slow fire over a history of you
reeling in the universe   Rhapsode
you and I have some walking to do, some
stitching together of the story so far, its feat
of silence, of sleeping lightly and listening
for the touch that outstrips all sense
in the hour before dawn   Look we have come
to the walled garden   See how the roses burn!
The lovers in the fountain spoon each other up
their drenched talk stretches the library resources
and when pubis and jawbone snick into place
you face my delight an uncontrollable smile

Returned Memory

— *Dinah Hawken*

This of course is a love poem.
Everything fits and is fitting:

the ground-plans, tempos, destinations:
the softest side of both bodies.

The treehouse

— *Anna Jackson*

Not having known the child
I love his graveyard,

the man who has grown up
over the child's bones,

the hair that springs like grass
from his shoulder blades,

the rise and fall of him,
the archaeology I disturb

late at night, asking him
for a story, as if we lay awake

in a treehouse, shining a torch
into the forest around us,

losing the beam
in the dark.

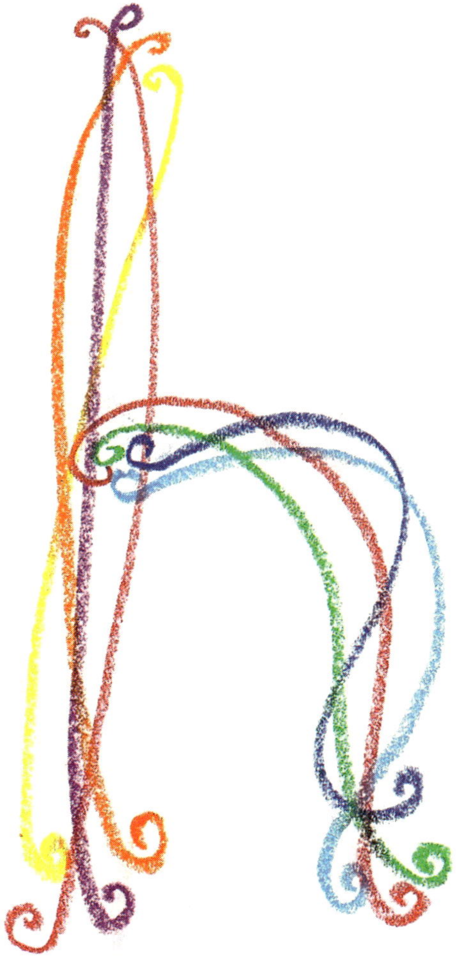

Change

— *A R D Fairburn*

Oh, were I turned all suddenly
    into a star,
in the cool wilderness of space
    to dwell afar;
or should they make of my body moondust,
    magical, white,
and scatter me about the silent roads
    of the world, at night;
or burn me in flame until I was but smoke
    upon the air . . .
still should my shadowy heart tremble a little,
    exquisitely,
at the words your voice spake, crying as of old
    in the dark to me.

Seven wishes

— *Fiona Farrell*

A straight account is difficult
so let me define seven wishes:

that you should fit inside me neat as the stuffing in an olive
that you should stand inside the safe circle of my eye
that you should sing, clear, on the high rock of my skull
that you should swing wide on the rope of my hair
that you should cross rivers of blood, mountains of bone
that I should touch your skin through the hole in your tee shirt
that we should exchange ordinary tales.

A Consort of Flower Parts

— *Gregory O'Brien*

for Jen

If the life of the mind is
a history of
interesting mistakes
    then what of

the life of the body — a memorable swim
within certain boundaries?

As in a botanical diagram,
letters are usually assigned
    the diverse parts:

stem, leaf, stamen, much the way
those same letters are dispersed
across the writerly sky
    above Hataitai.

So, too, our marriage was
annotated, inflected.
Let's go swimming, you said,
    in your blue shoes. Who needs

an ocean
or the blustery light

all about us. Afternoons
I returned to the suit
in which I was married,
    the blackness

of its incomparably blue
day — the sea of where it was
    we went.

    It was us, alone,
but not for long — others joined in,
names were distributed,
commas placed between them,
    bedrooms added,
instruments assigned.
Chandeliers hovered above
our time together,

letters of a glass alphabet. We thought
the world. And how it was we came to be
who we were

    or just west of there.
In the coral sea you were
the brightest of fishes
    and I was marooned
half way through a poem called
'Beauties of the Octagonal Pool'.

There were, at times, differences
concerning music, the lifespan
    of a couch, number of books
on a shelf, the time anything

takes. The year the Australian
Prime Minister wouldn't say 'sorry'
    we made a picnic
of the cold

but you were nowhere to be found
on that icy rug. We had driven
    down a side road
of the most organised greenness,
    at the end of which
a sign: 'Sorry, Garden Growing'.

It was the comma, carefully rendered,
that held us — this comma at the end of
    Hokianga Harbour,
high above Omapere, an eyelash
      or falling star. The comma

    after 'sorry'
which followed us south.
We thought the world

    of each other, and
beyond the bird-like lettering
    the cathedrals of
our time together

were a succession
    of photo-booths. Times
we forgot to smile.

It was Spring
or thereabouts
    and the high-flying punctuation
of Hataitai, all flower parts
and parts of speech, was
all about us. Out-of-service buses
bearing the word 'sorry'
    coasted by.

        With its dream of
perfectly spaced
events and objects, it is the comma
    that outlives these words — between

'sorry' and 'garden growing',
a seedling dropped
between adult plants. Whatever else
the season delivers

in the end all we have is
that
    which exists
between us, a pod and a curl,
which holds us
    together.

Found Again

— *Serie Barford*

our love is a tracking device
more sure than any global
positioning system

just carve us into wooden tablets
then imprint us on opposite corners
of a mighty length of siapo
and watch tusili'i spring forth

making bridges to connect us
over rock-bound starfish
scampering centipedes and
the footprints of bemused birds

we have many stories of
losing and finding each other

of getting lost
and losing others

but today all is well

I lie beneath the old mango tree
smothered with coconut oil
embellished with wild flowers
and droplets of your sweat

your aging shoulders
still fling back proud

and I still arch towards you
like a young sweetheart

you have whispered in my hair

found again

and we both know
this is our final harbour

siapo   bark cloth/tapa (Samoan)
tusili'i   fine or way lines used to connect individual
         designs (Samoan)

Birdsong

— *Sarah Broom*

if I cry like a bird,
listen for the pain
inside the pleasure,
if I shout out your name,
look for the dust
on the contours of my breath,
if I call you my lover,
turn your face away
and feel the air
supple on your skin,
the sun lingering
on the back of your neck,
if I say I will live
for a thousand years,
dig your feet in deep
and stand your ground,
if I move over you
like the gentlest of weathers,
look out to the water
and offer yourself
to the gods
of the outgoing
and incoming tides.

and if, after all,
when the world
starts to stray from me
like a grazing animal,
nonchalant, diverted,
frayed rope trailing,

if you are still here
and still listening,

then, if you can

sing to me

to Pru

— *Apirana Taylor*

we are a tree
our toes are roots
buried in the deep brown soil
we hold the sky up
in our branches
where the sunlight breaks through
on the buds
before the winds that blow
we are the ever green leaf

Urgently

— J C Sturm

for Jim

My dear one
And only dear
My moonrise
And early morning sun

When the time comes
Will you light my way
Through the dreaded fog
Of Hine-nui-te-po

And bring me safe
To that bright place
(I believe —
I swear I believe)
Where we may be together
Again, for ever.

Calculations

— *Kapka Kassabova*

The fire that lights a candle
cannot be shared between the wick
and the match, it has to be given
like a life.

The body lying on the wet sand
must leave an impression deeper
than the shallow water
coming to erase it.

May you never recover
from the lightness of my touch.

Letter home

— *Sam Hunt*

When things get too hard to bear
row out and catch the tide,
our blue dinghy stacked with beer;
ride the drift whichever way
as long as that long tide and half
the cold brown bottles last;
don't fear you'll ever be lost.

And if by the end of today
you catch the turned tide, love,
you'll be home, back in our bay,
the two black cats catching sprats,
gulls scavenging for the catch,
at the end of the first day
since they sent me away.

Love Affair

— Riemke Ensing

a given poem from Katherine Mansfield
with thanks to Helen McNeish

You wrote the table
was laid
for two
but nobody came
so you dined opposite
a white napkin.

It's called giving yourself
to life.
Through the window
a quiet branch
has the evening
to itself
also.

The photograph

— *Alison Wong*

So tell me how do you fall
out of love after so many years . . . slowly
imperceptibly . . . the way you walk
on the beach, luxuriously, just
like before, and forget to hold hands;
the way at night you stop coming
to wrap yourself round her in sleep

                          wrinkles
trace the skin one by one, each black hair
turns a shade off white, the light in your eye
grows darker than its pupil . . . you search
back to a fading photograph — catch
yourself falling out.

Ending and going home

— *Jenny Bornholdt*

Ending and going home
to where love
lives, high
above the town.

My favourite place,
where you find
sweet apples fallen
on the soft ground.

Watching the Motorway by Moonlight

— *Iain Sharp*

We sit on the viaduct
dangling our toes
in mid-air.
A truckload of turnips
heads towards Auckland
followed by
a carload of nuns
all eating hamburgers.
You close your eyes.
Your thoughts become
the night sky
the mist around the moon.
I nudge you gently.

Look, love, at the white moths.
An angel's wing is moulting.

warm loaf

— *Janet Charman*

warm loaf in my arms
it's time
to live in your name

i unswaddle you
hold this yam
fat and succulent
it fits your hand

beyond us
the grey roads glare
and my sister stands there
hand raised   good bye

we wave her   into oblivion
to school
the solid mother presence
beside me

we all leave soon

My Mother Dances

— *Albert Wendt*

Through the shadows cast by the moon tonight
the memory of my mother dances
like the flame-red carp I watched
in the black waters of the lake
of the Golden Pavilion in Kyoto.
Such burning grace.

Though I am ill with my future
and want to confess it to her
I won't. Not tonight.
For my mother dances
in the Golden Pavilion
of my heart.

How she can dance.
Even the moon is spellbound
with her grace.

Love poem for David

— *Selina Tusitala Marsh*

you are

my love, my life
my long time supporter
the father of my sons
(still waiting for my daughter)

you are

my inspiration
if you were Fiji
you'd be my holiday destination
if you were on a shop counter
you'd be the most expensive
if you were a spaghetti motorway junction
you'd be the most extensive
if you were a hotel
you'd be the Trump Towers
if we were on *Hart to Hart* you'd be Robert Wagner
to my Stefanie Powers

if you were a mountain
you'd be Everest
if you were olive oil
baby, you'd be hand pressed
if you were a cartoon
you'd be Superman

if we were picnicking at Onetangi, with lots of people,
and it started raining and thundering and there were no
cars or buses or shelter,
honey, you'd be the shuttle van

you are

my marathon runner
my true sparring partner
my basketball dribbler
my ear lobing nibbler
my fishing charter
my Red Sea parter

you are

by far the best looker
the last cube of sugar
my *Lord of the Rings* 'Precious'
the dish that's most delicious
you're the ace in the deck
you're the found shipwreck
you're the missing page
you're the last, intact shark cage
you're the winning Lotto ticket
you're the last chocolate biscuit
you're the trifecta
you're the finest flower's nectar

you are

my earth shaker
my deck maker
my builder, my designer,
my funny man one-liner
my stream in the wilderness
my one true kiss
my Boatshed Bay toaster
my Waiheke road coaster
my shared soulful laugh
my other half
my sun set and rise man
with you I can

you're the rock on which
I do all I do
and this poem, my love,
is to thank you.

Twelve Words Spoken by a Poem
— *Jill Chan*

If only I could
condense

and love like water
loves a vessel

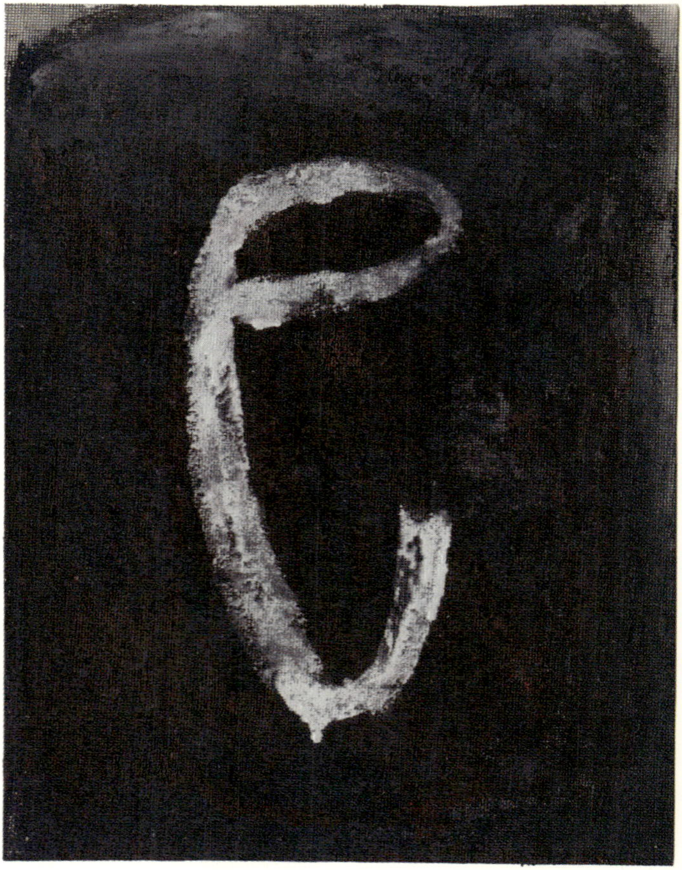

from Treasure Hunt

— *Mike Johnson*

Each morning we make a tunnel of time, dearest
and fall through the hours like bungy jumpers

hoping the thread will hold before we hit night, closing
our eyes against the impact. In the rush, children call

and other bodies twist around ours in their own medium
giving off smells and dreams and eyes and

hands. Each morning we strap ourselves into that faith
the night still sloshing through our heads and

clock the day running, fever fed from the rush
of the day before; and yet, when we hit

and the line around us tightens, we are flung
back through all our lives past and lives to come

head tearing open in the sudden, sheer
stillness.

*

The scoop of Palm Beach was dark as we walked
into the chill shadow of the headland. I was still

testing myself out in a new skin of feeling,
hesitant with joy in the open-ended

moonless night, and laughed;
for where we stopped and hugged we left our marks

in the sand, the scuffle of intimacy, for the next tide
to erase in the manner of philosophy, and felt

more blessed than our ordinary lives would credit
and well in flush with love. Returning we noted how

dark and soft the water was, like stroked fur,
how quietly the night lifted the spreading pohutukawa,

how lightly the sky bore its tide of stars and the thin
wandering line of foam.

The Voyage

— *Bill Manhire*

1
All night water laps
the hedges. I hold you in the middle
of the air.

2
Don't sleep
all night. It is pitch

black, but since
there is a vista, let

your throat be
the lantern.

3
Since there is
a window, let us

open it.

4
Let us dress
for a voyage. Let me

go out, with
your voice, to call for you.

See what a little moonlight can do to you?

— *Hone Tuwhare*

The moon is a gondola.
It has stopped rocking.
Yes. It's stopped now.

And to this high plateau
its stunning influence
on surge and loll of tides
within us should

somehow not go
unremarked
for want of breath
or oxygen.

And if I
to that magic micro-second
instant
involuntary arms reach out
to touch   detain

then surely
it is because you
are so good:
so very good to me.

Tell me you're waiting

— *Peter Bland*

Tell me you're waiting
at three in the morning
in your best silk dress
and that your skin
smells of Spring. Tell me
the children are sleeping
and the dark is listening
silently for my key
in the door. Tell me
it will always be this way
and that time passing
will repeat its rounds
and bring us together
again and again. Tell me
of love and other
miraculous meetings.
Tell me you're waiting,
knowing I'm almost there.

Free fall

— *Harry Ricketts*

for Will

Twenty years ago you
were born in blood, unfolded
like a parachute.

Now you call from Motueka
in tears. It's raining,
your girlfriend wants to live

day by day, your life's going
nowhere. I try to think
of something comforting,

reassuring: tomorrow's
another day; all relationships
hit rough patches; the thing's

to go with your own flow.
At this last — a phrase
I've picked up from you —

you start to splutter,
and soon we're laughing
at each other hysterically.

Coming and Going

— *Louis Johnson*

If love is what would make one offer himself
to bear the pains of another, there is so much
the baby does not understand I would gladly
stand in her stead for. But you cannot take
the pang for another or teach
pain quicker than the piercing thorn
any more than explain to the blind
the colour of blood or a bird.

Through glass of the kitchen door she watches
me return through the burning light of the day
and the indescribable sunset; her arms
suddenly wild signalling welcome.
What she makes of my comings and goings
I cannot guess or begin to explain.
Here one minute, gone another: small wonder
children find fathers incomprehensible
shadows, moon-ruled like tides, undependable.

Which is not why I pick her up from the floor —
but to secure for myself the fact of return
and the weight of the welcome. My fifty-odd
years are so close to a last departure
I know I should have thought harder
about such a new beginning. I tell myself
that love is quite as extreme as any entrance
or exit, and does not come too late. Its colour
glows in the room where I have closed the door.

The Bicycle

— *James Brown*

I have always been lucky.
When I was seven
my parents gave me
a red bicycle.

I rode it every day until
it became a part of me.

It had a basket on the front,
and my father attached a bell
to make doing the deliveries
more noticeable.

Pedalling up hills
pushed me so far inside my head
that only reaching the top
could bring me back out.

Going down, my mouth would open
as the world became flocks
of many-coloured birds
soaring into flight.

I loved that bicycle.

Lying in bed listening
to rain sheet against the window
and knowing that tomorrow
it was Monday,

I would get up and go
into the hall and stare at it,
consoled by the standing
of its beautiful silence.

Between

— *Rhian Gallagher*

Close in and distant, you had me.
Whichever way you moved
I was swept, arrested.

Between the stay of home
and flight, our poise,
our muddled disarray.

In greys of London light
mid-passage, on our walks
across Brooklyn Bridge

between one country and another
two zones to every hour.
Body into body, that fit,

between the letting go and hold,
your hand all night upon my hip.

viaduct

— Jen Crawford

a reward, a hand on the back on the small of the back.
walking out to a car. a night, a tiredness, a whisper.
your tiredness and that you did well.
building a wall around it. like a harbour with boats clinking.
like a sky, placed light and orange clouds.
the clubs and their liquid shout clinking.
your tiredness, your reward at the small of your back.

your reward the hand at the back of the thigh,
the edge of the skirt, & firm.
a rest. firm as the body of a car, a body of
decisions made by others for you to rest on.
door cell stamped from steel coil. wet
window against the back of your back
or. the hard turn.
resting in pressure.

let him watch, let him walk out to you
and watch. one close
as a hand as another watching
for your voice in
the symmetry of boats

At your visit

— *Joanna Margaret Paul*

(my voice too careless
& the light too bright)

a drawer, my
heart
long jammed
shut, falls

open

The Dance

— *Rhian Gallagher*

The apartment is small, a place of here
and now — two women step into a dance.
There isn't a moon or a star,
no reason at all.

This is our stomp and our whirl
swinging out and back,
this is our twofold orbit,
our rap. We writhe to the drum
and the rip; our moves
as makeshift as ever.

All our said and unsaid
grinds in our tread;
my heart races
like it did at the start.
We dance through the flames
and we dance in the ashes,
we give in this night
with all the sheer chance of our lives.

you are a hot -concentrate

— *Janet Charman*

you are a hot
concentrate   how will i
dissolve our detachment
unless by introducing you to my hand
to my left hand which
has all the subtlety of an advertisement divertissement
we may fall in love but surely
the old wounds will seal
and i will have your warm breath with my coffee
the little hairs and the long
there will be bitters and ginger to drink
and you sitting close as my finger
clothing
some on   some off never enough
the crumbled bed and our eating in all the languages at once
and more slowly
much more
slowly the six places to stoop and tie a shoe
to enter without knocking
to catch me in passing
to sit at a window while the street moves below the Frauenhaus
and you're cutting away my dear
cutting and shuddering in this room
adjacent smoke ferrying your scents
smoke bleeding across your arms and legs
unbuttoning an undistinguished front for the pudding
feel my
feel my two hands here

that will
distil the umbilical
as close as an eyeball
the therapeutic peripatetic clitoral literal peripheral lick
and mouths make decisions for nipples
and discussion and the words we wear
it's over here
address me

December

— *Sarah Quigley*

You arrived in the night
        quietly like the snow.

When I looked out
        the houses had been picked up
and put back down in a different
place.

Stairways were made beautiful.

The trees sang
        in small white voices,
people smiled.

Dog's body

— *Chris Price*

If this were child's play
and I could choose

I'd be the dog —
body a soft black curve

on the stone flags
of the square outside the gallery —

patient in my red collar
and tongue

all my love
in waiting.

Mute song

— *Kate Camp*

i

The first time I saw you
I don't know which I loved more
you with your tranquil neck
calmly transporting yourself through the world
or the one who followed you everywhere
trolling the dark waters like a hook.

ii

The strange thing was that
as each other's opposite and negative
we were even visible
I with my tatty winter coat
smelling of reeds
you consisting entirely of surfaces
or should I say one fabulously curved surface
smooth and white as an egg.

iii

I have no idea what you saw when you looked at me
a shadow dully pursued by the shape that cast it
a placeholder reserving a space from nonexistence.

Perhaps you saw God's fearsome ability
to be absent, his morosely taken option
to hoard his riches in another universe.

In anyone else, such a thought would be absurd.
In your case, it was luminous and adorable
shining in the dark location known as me.

iv

It was inevitable I would follow you
the sound of laughing that came
though you never laughed
the sweet nonsensical conversations
in which you remained impassively silent
the pointless journeys you took
your eyes perfectly round.

My desire was the desire to be superlative
I, who had spent years in domestic craft
became selfishly single-minded as an artist
inflicting your beauty on myself
like some ecstatic adolescent
cutting her arm with a pocket knife.

v

At night I would disappear.
You and the moon would glow.
I hated to think of the dark
covering you over like a mouth.

Picnic at Darkness Falls

— *James Brown*

The man and the woman enter the frame
quite unexpectedly, he holding out his hand
to help her over the rocks.
It is late summer and the river isn't full,
but even so the black water
lives up to its name. Little buffs of foam
spiral outwards from the roar of the falls,
like stars or galaxies, or at least
those slow revolving swirls
in TV animations of the night sky.
Heavenly bodies as webs of filmy
plasma; how do we know
what distance really looks like?
The woman spreads a blanket
and together they lay out the food.
Then they smile and stare around,
momentarily awkward,
as if the act of getting settled
has used up all they have to say.
If some words pass between them,
you and I aren't able to make them out.
They both look uncomfortably happy.
And we want to preserve that.
We do. Because . . . because of the
soluble nature of happiness.
And comfort's dull recline.
We never abandon our dreams,
we siphon them off.

It is late summer, but at this angle
and altitude the temperatures
are more like early spring
— warm in the sun,
but otherwise leafy and microbial.
Nevertheless, the insect population
knows heat when it's on offer
and is a canvas of activity:
butterflies veer for the light,
a spider sets off across
the surface tension.
The man removes his clothes
and scrambles onto a rock and
prepares to dive. The woman
reaches for a camera, zooming in;
her frame, our frame,
the whiteness of his neck.
Relationships must take more attention
than we ever imagine.
A finger's gentle pressure.
Click.

Remembering Summer

— *Brian Turner*

The memory of what you'd love to do again
    is on the rise. You'd run barefoot
over the grass on a summer's evening,

the sky like candy in the west
    where the wind and the sun die down,
watch light flickering in the bounce

of water flowing over a cobbly bed
    of gorgeous yellow, green and brown stones,
your mother's voice calling you home.

The gift

— *Peter Bland*

You love the new land
truly you love it
you pile up year
upon year until
belonging happens
and before you know it
the old land
drifts into myth
which you visit
disguised as a child

                the years

you left there
you can bring
to the new land
and offer them
as a gift
like a battered
old tomb vase
facing each new sunrise
by an open window
overlooking the sea

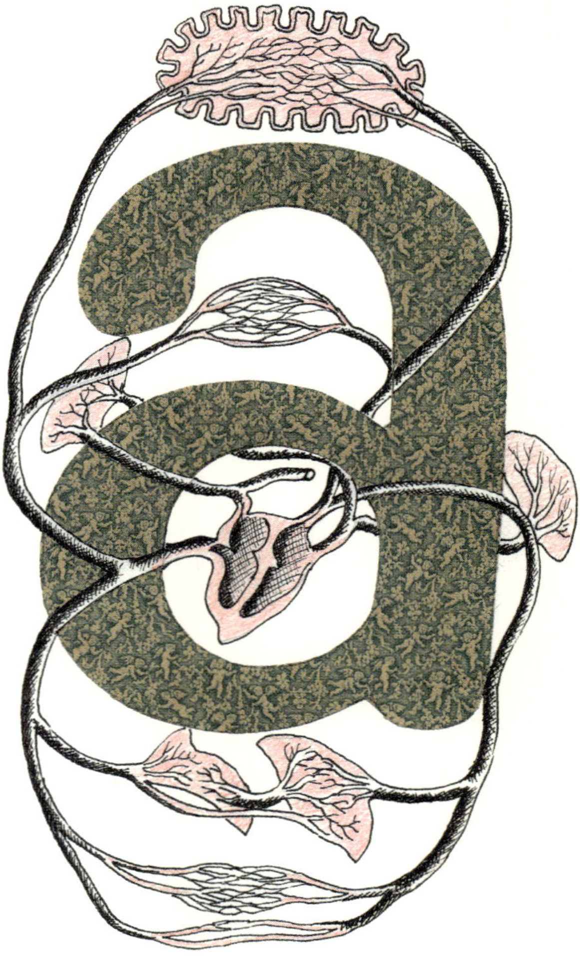

This is Love

— *Karlo Mila*

for David

you've taken / the roots of / my thoughts on / what love is /
this understanding I've created over the years /
so ripe / so red / in your big hands / brown / custodial

you put them in a pot / large bucket / on your front
doorstep / a place in the Papatoetoe sun / this is love you
say / watering / tending / a careful eye at the end of the day

it is seeds sown in the hopeful spring / hiccups of hope /
scattered sheets / seed spread bed / it is shedding dead leaves
in autumn / and you prune / me / cutting fingertips
tenderly / bleeding softly into soil / blistering gently / the
test is you say / whether we will survive winter / there
will be many winters / soaked with rain / frost on car
window mornings

this is love you say / endurance through every / every day /
  season

this is what I have learned.

love is not a bunch of red roses / blossomed into the peak
of their beauty / cut at the height of their passion / long
stemmed / bikini lined / full lipped / red perfect

love is / the watering / the watching / the pruning / the tending / the providing of new buckets / the finding of new door steps /

love is not something one simply wears
behind their ears
in full bloom

The Tides Run Up the Wairau

— *Eileen Duggan*

The tides run up the Wairau
That fights against their flow.
My heart and it together
Are running salt and snow.

For though I cannot love you,
Yet, heavy, deep, and far,
Your tide of love comes swinging,
Too swift for me to bar.

Some thought of you must linger,
A salt of pain in me,
For oh what running river
Can stand against the sea?

Lemon Tree

— *Owen Marshall*

Take this lemon tree and plant it
as some fond memory in your heart.
The Chinese profess the lemon is
Death's emblem, in our commerce it

denotes a worthless product, and
patriots see its hue as cowardice.
I say, take no notice of any such
sour history. Rather be my leman.

Conjure a fresh start, green foliage
and lamplit fruit. Take this gift,
this lemon tree, this smooth colour
and plant it as the sign I love you.

Portland Crescent

— *Anna Smaill*

Waking to the smell of frying bread,
the spiders on the ceiling,

that overhang
of corniced roses.

The sun shines
through baize curtains

past your hips
bowing them in radiance, like a martyr's.

The whole city's here for us;
there's a New World round the corner.

And I am here at last
and lying with you in this room

through the still and perfect morning
of the afternoon.

from The Bond of Time: An Epic Love Poem

— *John Puhiatau Pule*

Summer makes you laugh, and
you love swimming. You love what
I love; gulls, mountains, green
crushed fields, satin sheets, silk cushions;
you run from the rain that looks for you.

I hear you lament of black misfortunes,
stained with white sheets of our angry aura,
ritual of darkness; weep, weep,
stained and bruised lips; you fall
into oblivion and I weep, weep, weep.

You enter people's lives with bottles of
mineral water, collapsing from sheer
exhaustion of full summer days;
you come to watercress and parsley,
you peel oranges and slice apples.

This great misfortune of chopped laments
crushed both of us, and our eyes foam
fire of anger, jealousy and ugly words;
I see in you corpses of *tui* and cat,
and you settle for the breakage of my eyes.

We can rest on each other's belly; or walk
the mountain path that seems a wagon of
green apples; watch sunsets like a
peeled orange sink in fresh streams,
or murmur of other sunsets still remembered.

Deserts, for instance

— *Brian Turner*

The loveliest places of all
are those that look as if
there's nothing there
to those still learning to look

A Lullaby

— *Bill Manhire*

Here is the world in which you sing.
Here is your sleepy cry.
Here is your sleepy father.
And here the sleepy sky.

Here is the sleepy mountain,
and here the sleepy sea.
Here is your sleepy mother.
Sleep safe with me.

Here is pohutukawa,
here is the magpie's eye,
here is the wind in branches
going by.

Here is a heart to beat with yours,
here is your windy smile.
Here are these arms to hold you
for a while.

Here is the world in which you sleep,
and here the sleepy sea.
Here is your sleepy mother.
Sleep safe with me.

A Girl's Song

— *Ruth Dallas*

When love came
               glancing
                             down our street
Scarlet leaves
              flew
                    round our feet,

    sang the girl, sewing.

He told me
            he would
                      come again
Before
        the avenue
                turned green,

    sang the girl, sewing.

How could I know,
                or guess,
                        till now
The sadness
        of a
            summer bough,

    sang the girl, sewing.

Homage

— Ursula Bethell

I have told you much of the flowers in my garden
And many yet remain of which I have not told
But when I would tell you of the roses, the roses —
When it comes to the roses, how should I find words?

Yet to them I would consecrate a few faltering sentences
As they grow in their companies by colour and by kind.
Did I but enumerate the tale of chosen roses,
It would surely bring, to the chosen listener, joy.

Their names may be recorded but what record might be given
Of their symmetry, spell-binding scents, the depth
And gradual brilliance of eye-reposing hue?
No need, no need, when one speaks the word roses, roses,
All their beauty and significance is spoken too.

Roses of Persia, Roses of Damascus;
Roses held up for sale in Piccadilly Circus;
Roses for queens' bedchambers, and the costermongers' holiday;
Roses for the tender babe's first apprehensions
And for the sage's mystic contemplations;
Roses for marriage pomps, and the dear maid's untimely bier;
Roses for fame, pride, joy, romance,

Rapture, remembrance, solace in sore pain;
Symbols of secrecy, truth, love, holiness;
Roses on the green graves of our mortality,
Roses by the green walks of the New Jerusalem —

    So, to all you, my lovely roses, Hail.

The Grin

— *Keith Sinclair*

When I see a girl
quite absurdly happy
I think of you
coming to meet me.
Only those truly in love
smile that strange smile.
As a gannet,
wings fanned in the wind,
brakes on a nested rock
joyfully open-billed,
so I home in
to you with this wild grin.

from In Your Presence

a song cycle

— *Charles Brasch*

Far and far away,
Scent of a rose in the wind,
Your voice comes over the wires,

Smoke of mountain fires —
But you and no other, you,
Clear in the drift of day.

And oh, the heart's play,
Exulting of waters loosed,
As word with word conspires.

+

In love, what do we love
But to give and to receive
That love by which we live.

You, loved and known and unknown,
Are the one and only one
World I am chosen to dwell in.

I turn in your day and your night
Pivoting on one thought,
What we are and are not,

That love as evergreen mover
Is our always and our never,
Creator, destroyer, preserver.

Cassino *Città Martire*

— *Robert Sullivan*

Yet all I find are stones marking bones; stones
draped in paper poppies; stones shaped like men
in uniform; stones like broken graves stacked
into the abbey's holy renewal
with abbots' piety, vineyards and views
of the huddled city of martyrs' bones.

I sigh. I ask did I come too far? The
poet's eyes are upward past the mountain.
His eyes swim with Beatrice, a rippling
lustre swimming in heaven; I turn my
eyes from Māui's torn torso, his slashed blood
streaking the death goddess Hine's great thighs

as she holds his spirit like his body;
I cannot merely love the muse goddess
who crushed our PI hero in defence;
Beatrice strokes her hair now, and Hine's
barracuda teeth smile! The night goddess
holds our hero Māui's new spirit hand

like a baby's testing for reflexes
and Māui squeezes, and sucks the nipples
of Divine Hine, and flies winging out
to the leaping place with the world's last tree —
red blossoms pointing outward and upward
like colour behind an ear, combing scent

in the mind fixing atoms holding light
shaped in Beato Angelico's cells
who painted and held life's remembered light
so that a soul feels the weight of its life
and remembers its body, shakes dancing
in all its colours and so believing

decides to move up with courage past death
no longer bent-double but looking up
to what's unwritten — to more encounters
beyond the grave tears and release of death —
that our bones belong to stories of love
and in our loving we draw on their life.

Bouquet of Dead Flowers

— *David Eggleton*

Her body was braille, was scent bottles uncorked,
was the music score her breath hummed;
and beyond us the sun was the giggling Buddha,
robed in saffron, licking his finger
to tear months from the calendar.
The days withdrew from us like acupuncture needles
each morning when we woke up,
and slipped from the bedding seeking the promise
of orange juice you could take from the moment.
We sailed through seas of incense smoke together,
tranced by the gorgeous melodies of Indian-thighed summer,
by the gardens of wild poppies which grew all around us,
in the deserted volcanic quarries of the holiday season.
It seemed then that stereo speakers, always vibrating
their bongo heartbeat, busy bees in the calyx of a flower,
were the hypnotic metal portholes of our ship,
drumming its way through stormy passion.
Spiky juju crystals of the silence between us
were needed to calm that billowing passion,
and the dances we went to at night
only stirred it up, as the whole world duckwalked
with us, or were dirty dogs shaking down,
the brand-new leaves in that summer-of-love tree
fluttering on the breeze of yesterday's sound.

Of books and bookcases

— *Kiri Piahana-Wong*

My boyfriend says that
the one new thing he's
learnt about me since
we moved in together
is that I leave my
books lying around
all over the house.

It's true. I like to
be surrounded by
books, all their
different colours and
sizes, a wall of
words.

I tell him that the one
thing I've learnt about
him is that for a
cabinetmaker, he
doesn't own much
furniture.

I remind him of how
he won my heart by
promising to build me
bookcases for *all* my
books. He just

smiles, arranging the
books in towering
piles against the
wall.

The Fire is Lovely

— *Richard Langston*

To you whom I did love
to you whom I might love
to you whom I might have otherwise loved
to you that I do love
good evening, the fire is lovely.

the bird

— *Glenn Colquhoun*

My grandfather was a bird.

Underneath his white hair
he wore crayon-coloured feathers.

They were of boiling gold
and of burning red
and of drowning blue

One was green the colour of a single blade of grass.

When he walked ahead of me
I could see from his stride how he flew
in the branches of trees.

When his hand curled in my hair
I could feel him perching around me.

When he worked on the end of a shovel
I found how his arms spread wide in a turn.

And when he stood over a bed full of flowers
I saw that his eyes gathered what shone
on the ground for his nest.

When he was gone I remember him sitting in a tree
in a garden which he had planted.

And all the cries of morning were around him.

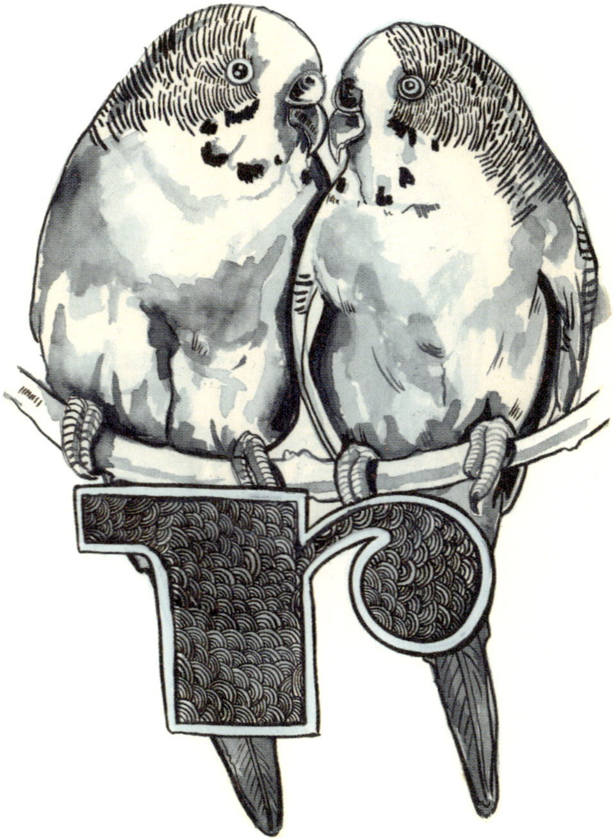

He Waiata mo Te Kare

— *James K Baxter*

1

Up here at the wharepuni
That star at the kitchen window
Mentions your name to me.

Clear and bright like running water
It glitters above the rim of the range,
You in Wellington,
I at Jerusalem,

Woman, it is my wish
Our bodies should be buried in the same grave.

2

To others my love is a plaited kono
Full or empty,
With chunks of riwai,
Meat that stuck to the stones.

To you my love is a pendant
Of inanga greenstone,
Too hard to bite,
Cut from a boulder underground.

You can put it in a box
Or wear it over your heart.

One day it will grow warm,
One day it will tremble like a bed of rushes
And say to you with a man's tongue,
'Taku ngakau ki a koe!'

3

I have seen at evening
Two ducks fly down
To a pond together.

The whirring of their wings
Reminded me of you.

4

At the end of our lives
Te Atua will take pity
On the two whom he divided.

To the tribe he will give
Much talking, te pia and a loaded hangi.

To you and me he will give
A whare by the seashore
Where you can look for crabs and kina
And I can watch the waves
And from time to time see your face
With no sadness,
Te Kare o Nga Wai.

5

No rafter paintings,
No grass-stalk panels,
No Maori mass,

Christ and his mother
Are lively Italians
Leaning forward to bless,

No taniko band on her head,
No feather cloak on his shoulder,

No stairway to heaven,
No tears of the albatross.

Here at Jerusalem
After ninety years
Of bungled opportunities,
I prefer not to invite you
Into the pakeha church.

6

Waves wash on the beaches.
They leave a mark for only a minute.
Each grey hair in my beard
Is there because of a sin,

The mirror shows me
An old tuatara,
He porangi, he tutua,
Standing in his dusty coat.

I do not think you wanted
Some other man.

I have walked barefoot from the tail of the fish to the nose
To say these words.

7

Hilltop behind hilltop,
A mile of green pungas
In the grey afternoon
Bow their heads to the slanting spears of rain.

In the middle room of the wharepuni
Kat is playing the guitar, —
'Let it be! Let it be!'

Don brings home a goat draped round his shoulders.
Tonight we'll eat roasted liver.

One day, it is possible,
Hoani and Hilary might join me here,
Tired of the merry-go-round.

E hine, the door is open,
There's a space beside me.

8

Those we knew when we were young,
None of them have stayed together,
All their marriages battered down like trees
By the winds of a terrible century.

I was a gloomy drunk.
You were a troubled woman.
Nobody would have given tuppence for our chances,
Yet our love did not turn to hate.

If you could fly this way, my bird,
One day before we both die,
I think you might find a branch to rest on.

I chose to live in a different way.

Today I cut the grass from the paths
With a new sickle,
Working till my hands were blistered.

I never wanted another wife.

9

Now I see you conquer age
As the prow of a canoe beats down
The plumes of Tangaroa.

You, straight-backed, a girl,
Your dark hair on your shoulders,
Lifting up our grandchild,

How you put them to shame,
All the flouncing girls!

Your face wears the marks of age
As a warrior his moko,
Double the beauty,
A soul like the great albatross

Who only nests in mid ocean
Under the eye of Te Ra.

You have broken the back of age.
I tremble to see it.

10

Taraiwa has sent us up a parcel of smoked eels
With skins like fine leather.
We steam them in the colander.
He tells us the heads are not for eating.

So I cut off two heads
And throw them out to Archibald,
The old tomcat. He growls as he eats
Simply because he's timid.

Earlier today I cut thistles
Under the trees in the graveyard,
And washed my hands afterwards,
Sprinkling the sickle with water.

That's the life I lead,
Simple as a stone,
And all that makes it less than good, Te Kare,
Is that you are not beside me.

Lyric

— *Michael Steven*

for Emma

The morning
was a palimpsest —
worn through by rain.
Our cups of tea
cooling on the desk.
Your hair spread
like pale fire
across the pillow's
dark ridges.

light

— *Alison Wong*

he moves his hand
down the dip of her back
over her buttocks
then up again
each stroke
the sound of a wave
over shingle
it's like your skin has a grain he says
like the scales of a fish
oh she says feeling the world turn
liquid
she turns and there
it is — a touch
of rainbow in her skin
as he catches her
in the right
light

Aunty Huia

— *Glenn Colquhoun*

I return from her house with the idea of her fingers. They are thin and black — the roots of pohutukawa. I am careful where I carry them in case they pinch.

I return from her house with the sound of her voice. There are sharp words left on the end of her sentences. Two I prise from my skin where they have stuck.

I return from her house with the smell of flax. It presses in an old book. When I open it again the leaves smell sweet as well as stale. For a moment I look around.

I return from her house with a piece of sky — that cloud which sits like a curled-up dog above her roof. The sound of barking comes from inside as I run.

I return from her house with the shape of her face. I carry it outstretched along the grass as though it is a pot of boiling water. At home I find a picture in a book of a roman emperor.

I return from her house with the taste of bread. My mouth walks round inside itself the way that people look at art inside a gallery. Butter runs against my tongue like wet paint.

I return from her house with the impression of her feet. They are as practical as hands. Her footsteps prepare the ground for walking as if they were plaiting long hair.

I return from her house with a piece of flax — to loop between the parts of her which I have left and carry them like car-keys in my hand — the way she carries a catch of snapper back home, at night, along the beach.

The Inner Life

— *Jenny Bornholdt*

I share a bed
with my husband,
an asthma puffer,
and often, under the pillows,
two pens. Life has never been
so good. In the morning
I get up and there are the cups
and saucers — one always to go
with the other.
I feel lucky to know
what a cup of flour
feels like. The way
this flour, with water,
can become bread.
With egg, cake.

Love in the Jam-maker's Mansion

— James Norcliffe

All in all it seemed love was the best option
in a time of drought with the people
praying for rain and the lakes shrinking
to scabs though the glossy leaves of citrus
shone through gusts of dust and grapefruit
glowed with the promise of marmalade.

In the dry wind, in the sound of flax clapping,
in a tinkle of glass bells it seemed best to open
the window to let the floral curtain billow
and blossom, let the large bed be our orchard
dangling with flesh and drooping with juice,
drupes fat with summer and lemon-light

all fructose and pectin-ready to set slowly
in polished bottles with elegant labels;
the sort you find in the saffron-scented
shops of the purveyors of fine comestibles,
conserved preserved for rainy seasons
jellied golden and sealed with red wax.

Later in a new morning we will walk
hand in hand down the creaking stairs
past the wide-eyed girls in white pinafores,
the men in grey waistcoats, to the green
portico and the stillness of a deserted lawn,
a broken fountain and parched distant hills.

Wide open spaces

— Lynn Davidson

You've read *Little House on the Prairie* —
you know the heart's acre when you see it.

Hidden in swaying grass the little house —
doors hinged with animal hide — secure but not fast.

You think of the girl who wanted to ride bareback
across the prairie — her hair flying loose.

You stride towards the house through grass that folds forward
like a ballerina, or a million ballerinas.

The howling wind is just
a fact of life.

At Scorching Bay

— *Bernadette Hall*

running the 'I-loves'
like kites along the shoreline

where the gulls startle
and rise

the sky shrinking

the clouds moving faster
than anything

Barbara

— Bob Orr

As if it were
an Oriental opium seat
I recline my head
on the small of your back.
And there off some spellbound coast
the crew of my body's ship
on the deck
one by
one
fall asleep in hammocks.
There they dream
without fear
of sailing
right off
        the edge of the world.

Love in the Dark Country

— *Kapka Kassabova*

Tomorrow for twenty-four hours
I'll be in the same country as you.

The sky will be constantly shifting,
the morning will be green, a single morning
for my single bed. And in the night

as the dark country goes to sleep
a church bell will measure
the jet-lag of my heart.

I'll open my suitcase
and unfold my life like a blanket.
In the dark country I will lie

all night and wonder how this came to be:
the one light left in the world
is your window, somewhere in this land

of thin rain and expensive trains,
and instead of maps
I have an onward ticket.

Tryst

— *Sue Wootton*

Museum of Modern Art, New York

She leans several angles at once, is all planes of Picasso,
tilting. How will she stand, her six-sided shins,
her five-walled thighs? How will she talk, one lip a cylinder
and one a box? Her tongue is a skewed guitar;
her three unblinking eyes dropped bombs, falling. He
is a handsome proportion of blue, was mixed on a Matisse palette
and is gaze upon gaze from his frame a window
onto all astoundingness, such blue truth. So he comes to her
who is all quaked scaffolding, shifted. Like sapphire,
cobalt ink, like tide, like midnight over Lapland in July,

like withheld rain is how he comes to her, and takes
her fractured fingers in his blue kiss. Now they spend their small hours
in the waterlilies, wading from one end of the triptych to the other, through
blurred and purpled Monet-water, setting the cerises rocking, rocking.

She and Her First Best Boyfriend

— *Dinah Hawken*

The night before, all through the night before, she and her first best boyfriend are kneeling with their hearts literally held together, whole-heartedly happy. They are two open books placed carefully against each other so that the words shift and mingle to make two new stories.

Makara

— Joan Fleming

That night, she tried to fit the whole of him
into the space of her and it hurt but in that good way
like when the stars in the back of your eyes explode
and you can finally see a path to the moon
and the moon is saying *oh oh oh* stroking the tide in.
They drove his van into the dark with the bed
in the back and five curtains with a pattern of flowers
so small at first they seemed like polka dots, or sometimes
not there at all. He kept stones everywhere
and she talked about the boulders she had seen
with hollows that would fit a human body
and he said *yes yes yes* and she picked one up
and so smooth she thought he *must* have loved them,
and also driftwood on the dashboard and strange
wheaty parachute tufts that could slow
a free-falling finger, maybe a whole hand.
Over the dark hills new to her and white angry signs
along the way, she didn't know about the wind farm
but he would always point to these things,
like later, in a friend's hallway he pointed to a map of Belize
and said *you know?* and she felt small
and said *no no no*. And they kept on the dark roads,
roads that later she could bike the whole way up
after saying for years she'd never bike in this town,
he was always the one disappearing down the path
of their house in his bright yellow cycling jacket,
he was always asking her to name the precise colour
of that exact patch of sky, getting out three pages

of computer paper to make a border and she would say
nothing is independent but would name it peach-grey
anyway. When they came to the beach they drove right
onto the sand and she leaned up against the van feeling
everything was possible and she was thin and her smile
was a whole sky and he grabbed her and pulled her into his beard
and said *I think I'm falling in love with you* but then later
he never said I'm falling in love with you.
That's the thing about possibility. Anyway,
they chased each other across the dark beach
like children and hardly slept in the tin van home
under his clever netting with its small light and
its insect repellent and its holes. In the daylight
they were parked ten metres from someone's front porch
where a man was having his morning coffee, they hadn't seen
the distance in the dark but he said he didn't care
he would make love to her with all the windows open
and the sun on his back, but of course he didn't, and
they dressed each other, boiled their own thick morning cup
on the camp stove and talked about going to the Orongorongos,
and what it might be like, and what it might be like to stay.

Cherries

— *Renee Liang*

In summer we bought
cherries
taut black bags
of juice-splurged sweetness

filling bag
after handpicked bag —
look, I'd say
twins

I've got triplets
you'd reply —
you were always
so damned competitive.

Back home
(cherries by the handful
tumbled under tapwater &
plopped into mouths, whole)

back home
the real contest would begin.
Look, mine's bigger
I'd claim

no, *mine's* bigger
you'd say —
watch, I'll tie a loop
in the stalk with my tongue.

And so we'd tangle
in lingual gymnastics
until someone
won

a knot
tied neatly
on our tongues,
meaning

we'd find true love
at last.

Newborn

— *Emma Neale*

His mouth a small red hearth
we huddle around:
forest creatures drawn
to its light and warmth.

When its suck and flicker at the breast stops
we blow cool breath on the soft black coal of his head
to make its wet spark dart again.

A scarlet trapdoor with tiny clapper
that knocks and knocks at our dreams and enters,

his mouth springs open
like the lid of a surprise
to loosen translucent birthday balloons of

Ah, ah.
I, I.

We stand here and watch them rise;
the night crowds at fireworks
make of our own mouths a kind of mirror:

Oh. Oh. You.

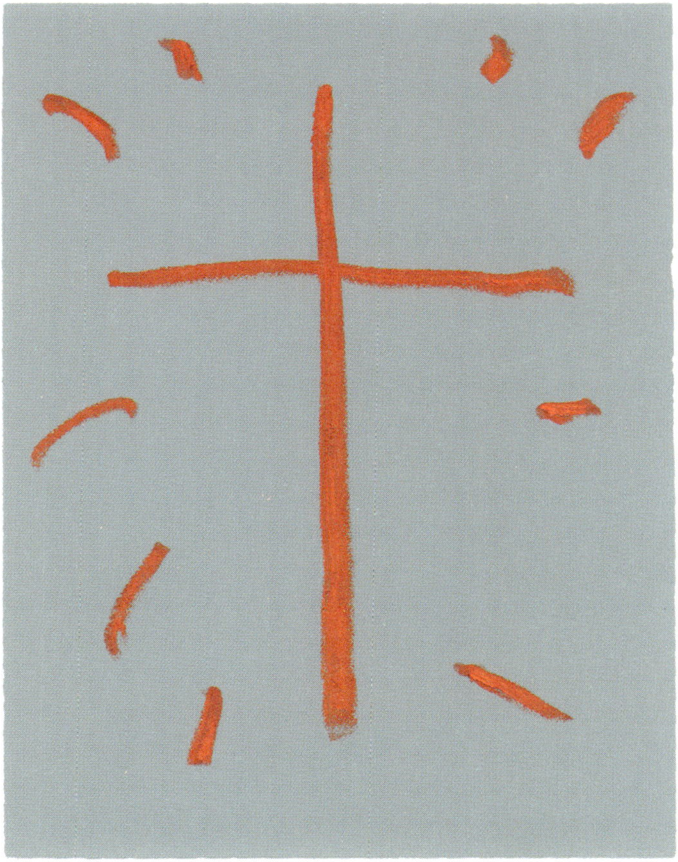

On a Son Returned to New Zealand

— *Fleur Adcock*

He is my green branch growing in a far plantation.
He is my first invention.

No one can be in two places at once.
So we left Athens on the same morning.
I was in a hot railway carriage, crammed
between Serbian soldiers and peasant
women, on sticky seats, with nothing to
drink but warm mineral water.
                                           He was
in a cabin with square windows, sailing
across the Mediterranean, fast,
to Suez.
            Then I was back in London
in the tarnished summer, remembering,
as I folded his bed up, and sent the
television set away. Letters came
from Aden and Singapore, late.
                                          He was
already in his father's house, on the
cliff-top, where the winter storms roll across
from Kapiti Island, and the flax bends
before the wind. He could go no further.

He is my bright sea-bird on a rocky beach.

August

— *Stephanie Johnson*

Before the walk, on either side of Willa's pram, we fasten
down the domes. Rain threatens all the way
but she laughs, hood back,
laughs at the threatening sky,
all gums.

In bursts the sun is hot,
almost spring. Maeve reaches
her small arms into gardens, contemplates
picking the furthermost flower.

On the corner our boy waves
his wheels blur, the footpath is hard and cold
but miles below him — he's six years old
invincible for the moment.
He vanishes, pedalling fast.

After the turn we will see him.
He will be there, poised,
a small figure in the dusk,
waiting, impatient, flushed.

> You and I, my love, are the wheeless ones,
> a word here and there,
> a steadying hand.
> We are their moving landmarks,
> points of return,
> two towers of light in the darkening streets.

Auckland, 1994

Silly

— *Meg Campbell*

I am stepping over the dogs to reach you
in the kitchen. While your back's turned
I'll grip you in my arms (which are like
the legs of a jumping spider). When you
turn and fend me off, shoo-ing me
to a safe distance, you purse your lips
for a kiss, and 'THAT'S THAT!' you snap.
'IT'S LOVE!' I think. One day
I'll swing you over my head
on to the bed, and steal twenty dollars
from your wallet, and sit on you
until you cry 'MERCY' and
'I LOVE YOU WITH THE LOVE
OF A JUMPING SPIDER' which is hard
and shiny, and I'll step backwards on to
the dogs, who'll shriek, and we'll be
united in soothing their feelings.
Why is it so sweet to me — you
in the kitchen, and me at arm's length?
Silly.

6 The Eternal Sunshine of the Spotless Mind

— *Helen Rickerby*

from Nine Movies

I'm pretty sure I know now
what love tastes like
and it takes something so
fantastical
to balance the sweet sharp salt
the corners of your tongue
to wash away the sticky syrup
that gets on my hands
and makes it hard to think

Running through the passages, tunnels of us
all made of books, stacked floor-
to-ceiling, and if they should topple
we'd be trapped beneath Brontës and Eliots
Dostoyevskys, Tolstoys
Atwoods and Couplands and Greenes
Living in constant danger of being crushed
by the weight of Western literature
is just one of the risks we take

I know there are rooms inside of me
that you've never been to
You've whole basements
you've locked yourself out

I Love Those Photos

— *Vivienne Plumb*

I love those photos I took in '79 in the desert,
all sky, red sand and dust at sunset.
And one gumleaf pressed flat in a book,
curled like a crescent moon
pink and green. Last night, I dreamt
I broke it, the smell of eucalyptus
crumbling in my hand.
Me making homemade jam, marmalade
and relish, glowing like fists of jelly
jewels in clean clear jars.
And that night we stayed up really late,
got drunk, and thought we might
ring up people we hate and
make funny noises down the phone.
I laughed, and then we lit the candles again
on your birthday cake, and you bent forward
and blew, and then it was black,
and in the darkness, I just touched you.

The Messenger
— *Joanna Preston*

Not a postcard, or a tease
of lace.
In my absence I send
a strange messenger, my love
but true —

I send a spoon.

Its haft slips into your hand
gladly, like mine,
returns the faint warmth
of fingers and thumb

helpful as a wife.

The curve of its bowl
against your lips —
know this
for the bow of mine

let it rest there
the winter moon's reflection
reaching across a lake,
across the night's dark throat

it scents
everything you taste.

And at night
it will nestle in the drawer
and croon its song of longing

to the quiet house
to our half-empty bed.

jill

— *Brian Potiki*

there's one thing that keeps me
from the whare porangi —
the thought that one day
i might own a battered lime-green volvo
& three things that keep me
from my grave —
the grandchild who astounds me with her poetry
the feckless love of humanity i get
from a second glass of guinness
your love
like
rain
on
a
green
leaf

dear heart

— *Michele Leggott*

dear heart it was a coast road
long past lilac time and well out of town
                       the sea out of sight   and driving north
                     in the far south the radio swelled
         nostalgia
         and I want you to know
                       that I remember it all   the time
   it was 'just' part of your afternoon repertoire
   a dance-floor pick-up
         kept on at you all those years   the romance the real
         life dance we were brought in to share
     the sun and the son
     you were making it true with a late-fifties step
                   up the coast   into heaven
         and some memorable parties
         fishing trips
                carnivals
                      a dog   a truck   a baby sister
    a walk to the swing bridge
  and back
    and more . . .

then it was moving into town   settling
             down and later the piano
                          you were picking out Mancini arrangements
Nat King Cole My Fair Lady and the theme
from Mondo Cane
             you sang them into the woodwork
             and when it really was
                          a table for one and a single rose
                          that hard lost time
   I heard Errol Garner play I only
have eyes for you in a winter house   dancing
                          with knots in my throat past midnight
                and your brave tra-la-la
   half a world away
                it's a lonely thing to do
                and you couldn't get used to the cold
                                or the hole in the bed
                   the silence after you sang out
                   the songs that would never mean dancing again
   oh my sentimental mother

you died
and I saw you in each other's arms again
                            an hour from dawn
      just as it should have been
   my dear

   I took your rings and came back to the real
   life dance of these years
               a song by songs and it seems I don't know all the words
               because you never did
                          but
  here we are driving the coasts of our dreams and
  bending again in time
              over the precious cradle of the heart

from The Time of the Giants

— *Anne Kennedy*

In the water they cling with all the pieces of their bodies
fitting and floating in the breaking sunlight
broken up as if by a system of mirrors
buried already like Egyptian nobles together
with all their fine smiles
and the bangles of their shouted
sweet-talk.
Their shouts come bouncing eagerly across the water
walking on water etc also sine waves and cosine.
How it's all connected!
(How the sky is given its blue.)

Now he's laughing her into. Let's race. Quest. No. Yes.
Don't, she says, I warn you. He says Oh you're
warning me are you! Seriously she could beat
anyone. It's her length and her enormous
buoyancy in the water, where everything
is turned on its head, inside out
heavy is light and full of shadows is
empty. Not that she tells him that.

But as they swim he throws apples in her path
which aren't really apples of course but
the bloodshed of his smiles. She loves them so.
She must stoop to collect each one

and she loses
and he wins and she doesn't of course
mind.

Next she's going to do it stand she's going to
stand and he will love her and he will
still love her.

Let's be honest here
— *J C Sturm*

I know and you know
The play could have
A different cast
Playing our parts
And be as good or better.

You could be someone else
And I would hold and love him
Like this and this, whisper
Extravagances
Like these and mean them.

Or I could be another
Leading lady
And you would study
Face and form closely
As always,

Learn to use her name
Like Open Sesame,
And she would hear you
In a dream
As I do now, and smile.

For Thee

— *Hone Tuwhare*

If I thought your usual blue smile
   today was greyer, I'd check it out
   with the inscrutable skies above,
   who — without batting a cloudless
   eyelid, would let me have my
   own autonomy to decide for myself
   whether a storm was building, or
   clear skies were on offer. But
   I have a problem with this.

You see, I much prefer to be
   sitting in front of a huge
   fireplace — with a log-fire crackling,
   light & heat from it, warming me;
   & licking my face; a palette of
   golden colours shaping
   the taste, the smell and texture
   of my dream of you. You, my
   darling . . . you.

Catch

— *Murray Edmond*

Two sitting at a table
two at a table sitting
two and two
a table in the grass
in the grass a table
and two two at table
and on the table
empty almost with a little
a little empty almost but
with a little water
there sits a jar for love
on the table a jar for love
not a fresh jar every day
fresh every day
nothing in the jar that lasts
always fresh they are sitting
sitting at the table
looking they are looking
at the jar at the table
at each other they are
sitting looking sitting
at the table at the jar
looking looking sitting
now is nearly the day
the day is nearly now now
go to sleep go to love
go to jar go to look

look looking look
sit sitting catch that catch
two sitting at a table
two at table sitting
two and two and two
a table in the grass

Acknowledgements

Grateful acknowledgement is made to the following poets and copyright holders for permission to reproduce these poems:

Fleur Adcock 'On a Son Returned to New Zealand' *High Tide in the Garden* (London: Oxford University Press, 1971)

Angela Andrews 'Son' *Echolocation* (Wellington: Victoria University Press, 2007)

Hinemoana Baker 'Time of Day' *mātuhi | needle* (Wellington: Victoria University Press, 2004)

Serie Barford 'Found Again' *Tapa Talk* (Wellington: Huia Publishers, 2007)

Sarah Jane Barnett 'The Apple Picker' (previously unpublished)

James K Baxter 'The Beach House' *Pig Island Letters* (London: Oxford University Press, 1966) 'He Waiata mo Te Kare' *Autumn Testament* (Wellington: Price Milburn, 1972)

Airini Beautrais 'Love Poem for a Love a Long Time Ago' 'Love Poem for the Tauherenikau River' *Western Line* (Wellington: Victoria University Press, 2011)

Ursula Bethell 'Homage' *From a Garden in the Antipodes* writing as Evelyn Hayes (London: Sidgwick & Jackson, 1929)

Peter Bland 'Bear Dance' *Mr Maui* (London: London Magazine Editions, 1976) 'Tell me you're waiting' 'The gift' *Coming Ashore* (Wellington: Steele Roberts, 2011)

Jenny Bornholdt 'Ending and going home' 'Wedding song' *How We Met* (Wellington: Victoria University Press, 1995) 'The Inner Life' *The Hill of Wool* (Wellington: Victoria University Press, 2011)

Charles Brasch from 'In Your Presence' *Ambulando* (Christchurch: Caxton Press, 1964)

Diana Bridge 'Life eternal' *Red Leaves* (Auckland: Auckland University Press, 2005)

Bub Bridger 'Wild Daisies' *Wild Daisies: The Best of Bub Bridger* (Wellington: Mallinson Rendell, 2005)

Sarah Broom 'because' 'Birdsong' (previously unpublished)

Diane Brown 'talk about a tonic' *Learning to Lie Together* (Auckland: Godwit, 2004)

James Brown 'Picnic at Darkness Falls' *Lemon* (Wellington: Victoria University Press, 1999) 'The Bicycle' *The Year of the Bicycle* (Wellington: Victoria University Press, 2006)

Kate Camp 'Mute Song' *The Mirror of Simple Annihilated Souls* (Wellington: Victoria University Press, 2010)

Alistair Te Ariki Campbell 'Words and Roses' from 'Cages For the Wind' *Gallipoli & Other Poems* (Wellington: Wai-te-ata Press, 1999)

Meg Campbell 'Silly' *Resistance* (Paekakariki: Earl of Seacliff Art Workshop, 2005)

Jill Chan 'Twelve Words Spoken by a Poem' *Early Work: Poems 2000–2007* (Charleston: Createspace, 2011)

Janet Charman 'warm loaf' *Red Letter* (Auckland: Auckland University Press, 1992) 'you are a hot -concentrate' *End of the Dry* (Auckland: Auckland University Press, 1995)

Glenn Colquhoun 'Aunty Huia' 'the bird' *The Art of Walking Upright* (Wellington: Steele Roberts, 1999)

Jen Crawford 'viaduct' *Napoleon Swings* (Auckland: Soapbox Press, 2009)

Wystan Curnow '[but you]' *Back in the USA: Poems 1980–82* (Wellington: Black Light Press, 1989)

Ruth Dallas 'A Girl's Song' *Country Road and Other Poems, 1947–52* (Christchurch: Caxton Press, 1953)

Lynn Davidson 'Wide Open Spaces' *Sport 39* (2011)

Eileen Duggan 'The Tides Run Up the Wairau' *Poems* (London: Allen & Unwin, 1937)

Lauris Edmond 'The nervous public speaker' *A Matter of Timing* (Auckland: Auckland University Press, 1996)

Murray Edmond 'Catch' *Fool Moon* (Auckland: Auckland University Press, 2004)

David Eggleton 'Bouquet of Dead Flowers' *Rhyming Planet* (Wellington: Steele Roberts, 2001)

Johanna Emeney 'Tipple Over Tail' *Apple & Tree* (Auckland: Cape Catley, 2011)

Riemke Ensing 'Love Affair' *The K. M. File and Other Poems with Katherine Mansfield* (Christchurch: Hazard Press, 1993)

A R D Fairburn 'Change' *He Shall Not Rise* (London: Columbia Press, 1930)

Fiona Farrell 'Seven wishes' *Cutting Out* (Auckland: Auckland University Press, 1987) 'The castle' (previously unpublished)

Joan Fleming 'Makara' *Sport 36* (2008) 'Husband and Wife Talk Without Talking at a Difficult Dinner Party' *The Same as Yes* (Wellington: Victoria University Press, 2011)

Janet Frame 'Before I Get into Sleep with You' 'Child'

The Goose Bath: Poems (Auckland: Vintage, 2006).
Copyright is held by the Janet Frame Literary Trust.

Rhian Gallagher 'Between' 'The Dance' *Shift* (Auckland: Auckland University Press, 2011)

Denis Glover 'Brightness' *To a Particular Woman* (Christchurch: Nag's Head Press, 1970)

Paula Green 'Glenburn' *Crosswind* (Auckland: Auckland University Press, 2004)

Bernadette Hall 'lovesong' 'wedding song' *The Merino Princess: Selected poems* (Wellington: Victoria University Press, 2004) 'At Scorching Bay' *The Ponies* (Wellington: Victoria University Press, 2007)

Michael Harlow 'Billet-doux' *The Tram Conductor's Blue Cap* (Auckland: Auckland University Press, 2009)

Dinah Hawken 'She and Her First Best Boyfriend' *Small Stories of Devotion* (Wellington: Victoria University Press, 1991) 'Returned Memory' 'The Verb to Give' *One Shapely Thing: Poems and Journals* (Wellington: Victoria University Press, 2006)

Jeffrey Paparoa Holman 'As big as a father' *As Big as a Father* (Wellington: Steele Roberts, 2002)

Ingrid Horrocks 'My Mother's Voice' *Mapping the Distance* (Wellington: Victoria University Press, 2010)

Sam Hunt 'A new plateau song' 'Letter home' *Doubtless: New & Selected poems* (Nelson: Craig Potton, 2008)

Robin Hyde 'Embrace' *Young Knowledge: The Poems of Robin Hyde* (Auckland: Auckland University Press, 2003)

Kevin Ireland 'Inventing You' *How to Survive the Morning: New Poems* (Auckland: Cape Catley, 2008) 'The Wish' *Table Talk: New Poems* (Auckland: Cape Catley, 2009)

Anna Jackson 'Fontanello' 'The treehouse' *Catullus for Children* (Auckland: Auckland University Press, 2003)

Louis Johnson 'Coming and Going' *Coming & Going* (Wellington: Mallinson Rendel, 1982)
Mike Johnson from 'Treasure Hunt' *Treasure Hunt* (Auckland: Auckland University Press, 1996)
Stephanie Johnson 'August' *Moody Bitch: Poems of the last two decades* (Auckland: Godwit, 2003)
Andrew Johnston 'The Sounds' *The Sounds* (Wellington: Victoria University Press: 1996)
Kapka Kassabova 'Calculations' *Someone Else's Life* (Auckland: Auckland University Press, 2003) 'Love in the Dark Country' *Geography for the Lost* (Auckland: Auckland University Press, 2007)
Jan Kemp 'Puriri' *The Sky's Enormous Jug: Love poems old and new* (Auckland: Puriri Press, 2001)
Anne Kennedy from *The Time of the Giants* (Auckland: Auckland University Press, 2005)
Fiona Kidman 'The ngaio tree' *Where Your Left Hand Rests* (Auckland: Godwit, 2010)
Richard Langston 'The Fire is Lovely' *The Trouble Lamp* (Wellington: Fitzbeck Publishing, 2009)
Michele Leggott 'dear heart' *Swimmers, Dancers* (Auckland: Auckland University Press, 1991) from '*dia*' and 'keeping warm' *Dia* (Auckland: Auckland University Press, 1994)
Renee Liang 'Cherries' (previously unpublished)
Anna Livesey 'Great Full Moon, Lowering Behind the Black Hill' *The Moonmen* (Wellington: Victoria University Press, 2010)
Iain Lonie 'A Late Honeymoon' *Winter Walk at Morning* (Wellington: Victoria University Press, 1991)
Rachel McAlpine 'Love Song' *Lament for Ariadne* (Dunedin: Caveman Press, 1975)

Cilla McQueen 'A Lightning Tree' *Axis: Poems and drawings* (Dunedin: University of Otago Press, 2001) first published in *Wild Sweets* (John McIndoe, 1986) 'The Language of Bluff' *Fire-Penny* (Dunedin: University of Otago Press, 2005)

Bill Manhire 'The Voyage' *The Elaboration: Poems* (Wellington: Square & Circle, 1972) 'Inesilla' *What to Call Your Child* (Auckland: Godwit, 1999) 'A Lullaby' *The Victims of Lightning* (Wellington: Victoria University Press, 2010)

Selina Tusitala Marsh 'Love poem for David' (previously unpublished)

Owen Marshall 'Lemon Tree' *Sleepwalking in Antarctica* (Christchurch: Canterbury University Press, 2010)

Karlo Mila 'This is Love' *Dream Fish Floating* (Wellington: Huia Publishers, 2005) 'For the father of my children' *A Well Written Body* (Wellington: Huia Publishers, 2008)

David Mitchell 'A Letter' *Steal Away Boy: Selected Poems of David Mitchell* (Auckland: Auckland University Press, 2010)

Emma Neale 'Newborn' 'Traveller overdue' *Spark* (Wellington: Steele Roberts, 2008)

James Norcliffe 'Love in the Jam-maker's Mansion' *Villon in Millerton* (Auckland: Auckland University Press, 2007)

Gregory O'Brien 'A Consort of Flower Parts' 'Love poem' *Beauties of the Octagonal Pool* (Auckland: Auckland University Press, 2012)

Bob Orr 'Barbara' *Valparaiso* (Auckland: Auckland University Press, 2002)

Joanna Margaret Paul 'At your visit' 'His eyes' 'Still Life' *Like Love Poems* (Wellington: Victoria University Press, 2006)

Kiri Piahana-Wong 'Of books and bookcases' (previously unpublished)
Vivienne Plumb 'I Love Those Photos' *Salamanca* (Wellington: HeadworX, 1998) 'I love peaches' (previously unpublished)
Brian Potiki 'jill' *Aotearoa: Collected poems and songs* (Wellington: Steele Roberts, 2003)
Jenny Powell 'Love in the Early Winter' *Hats* (Wellington: HeadworX, 2000) 'White Gold' *Four French Horns* (Wellington: HeadworX, 2004)
Joanna Preston 'The Messenger' *Takahe* 70 (Winter 2010)
Chris Price 'Dog's body' *Husk* (Auckland: Auckland University Press, 2002)
John Puhiatau Pule from *The Bond Of Time: An Epic Love Poem* (Suva: Pacific Writing Forum, 1998)
Sarah Quigley 'December' *Love in a Bookstore or Your Money Back* (Auckland: Auckland University Press, 2003)
Helen Rickerby '6 The Eternal Sunshine of the Spotless Mind' from 'Nine Movies' *Sport* 39 (2011)
Harry Ricketts 'Free fall' *Your Secret Life* (Wellington: HeadworX, 2005) 'Quarantine Island' (previously unpublished)
Jack Ross 'The Miracle' *Love in Wartime* (Wellington: Pania Press, 2006) 'After Apollinaire' *Tongue in Your Ear 5* (2001)
Iain Sharp 'Watching the Motorway by Moonlight' *The Pierrot Variations* (Auckland: Hard Echo Press, 1985)
Keith Sinclair 'The Grin' *The Firewheel Tree* (Auckland: Auckland University Press, 1973). Copyright is held by Raewyn Dalziel.
Anna Smaill 'Portland Crescent' *The Violinist in Spring* (Wellington: Victoria University Press, 2005)

Elizabeth Smither 'At the Beginning of Love' *Red Shoes* (Auckland: Godwit, 2003) 'Ruby's heirloom dress'

Charles Spear 'Audrey' *Twopence Coloured: Poems* (Christchurch: Caxton Press, 1951) Reissued by Holloway Press in 2007.

Mary Stanley 'Love by Candlelight' 'Puer Natus' *Starveling Year* (Auckland: Auckland University Press, 1994 [1953]). Copyright is held by Alexandra Smithyman.

C K Stead 'You' *The Red Tram* (Auckland: Auckland University Press, 2004)

Michael Steven 'Lyric' *Bartering Lines* (Dunedin: Kilmog Press, 2009)

J C Sturm 'Urgently' *Dedications* (Wellington: Steele Roberts, 1996) 'Let's be honest here' *Postscripts* (Wellington: Steele Roberts, 2000)

Robert Sullivan 'Arohanui' *Shout Ha! To the Sky* (London: Salt, 2010) 'Cassino *Città Martire*' *Cassino: City of Martyrs* Città Martire (Wellington: Huia Publishers, 2010)

Apirana Taylor 'to Pru' (previously unpublished)

Chris Tse 'Husband to Wife' *AUP New Poets 4* (Auckland: Auckland University Press, 2011)

Brain Turner 'Remembering Summer' *Taking Off* (Wellington: Victoria University Press, 2001) 'Deserts, for instance' *Just This: Poems* (Wellington: Victoria University Press, 2009) 'Dream' 'If She Hadn't Been There' *Inside Outside* (Wellington: Victoria University Press, 2011)

Hone Tuwhare 'See what a little moonlight can do to you?' *Mihi: Collected Poems* (Auckland: Penguin, 1987) 'For Thee' *Piggy-back Moon* (Auckland: Godwit, 2001)

'Poem for Kereihi' *Small Holes in the Silence: Collected Works* (Auckland: Vintage, 2011). Copyright and publishing rights are held by the Estate of Hone Tuwhare. honetuwhare@gmail.com

Ian Wedde 'To Utopias' *The Commonplace Odes* (Auckland: Auckland University Press, 2001)

Albert Wendt 'My Mother Dances' *Shaman of Visions: Poems* (Auckland: Auckland University Press, 1984)

Virginia Were 'Apartment' *Jump Start* (Wellington: Victoria University Press, 1999)

Alison Wong 'light' 'The photograph' *Cup* (Wellington: Steele Roberts, 2006)

Sue Wootton 'Tryst' *By Birdlight* (Wellington: Steele Roberts, 2011)

Sonja Yelich 'grahams beach, bach' *Clung* (Auckland: Auckland University Press, 2004)

Poet and artist biographies

Poet biographies

Fleur Adcock (1934–) was born in Papakura. She spent her childhood in England, returned to New Zealand at thirteen and, as an adult, settled permanently in London. She has produced fourteen volumes of poetry, several anthologies, and translations from Latin and Romanian. In 2006 her collection *Poems, 1960–2000* won the Queen's Gold Medal for Poetry.

Angela Andrews (1977–) was born in Rotorua. After graduating from medical school she worked for several years as a doctor, then completed an MA in Creative Writing at Victoria University. Her first collection, *Echolocation*, was published in 2007 and her poetry has appeared in various New Zealand journals, including *Best New Zealand Poems* in 2005 and 2007.

Hinemoana Baker (1968–) (Ngāti Raukawa, Ngāti Toa Rangatira, Te Āti Awa, Kāi Tāhu, Ngāti Kiritea England, Germany) is a poet, musician and playwright. She completed an MA in Creative Writing at Victoria University. She co-edited *Kaupapa: New Zealand poets, world issues*, has published two poetry collections, and has appeared in *Best New Zealand Poems* as well as numerous journals and anthologies.

Serie Barford (1960–) was born in New Zealand. She is a performance poet of Samoan, Celtic, Scandinavian and Algonquin Indian ancestry. She has worked as a school teacher and is now involved in community education. Her latest poetry collection is entitled *Tapa Talk*, and she is a member of Polynation, a Pacific-Island performance group.

Sarah Jane Barnett (1977–) is a writer and reviewer who lives in Wellington. Her work has appeared in a range of journals such as *Landfall*, *Sport*, *Turbine* and *Southerly*. Her poems were also selected for *Best New Zealand Poems* 2007 and 2010. Sarah is currently completing a creative writing PhD in the field of ecopoetics.

James K Baxter (1926–1972) was born in Dunedin and completed studies at university and teachers' college. In his short life, he accumulated a significant body of work that included poetry, plays, literary criticism, and social and religious writing. Baxter was the Burns Fellow (1966–67) and was married to the poet J C Sturm. Paul Millar (2010) and Sam Hunt (2009) have edited anthologies of his work.

Airini Beautrais (1982–) won the NZSA Jessie Mackay Award for Best First Book of Poetry in 2007 with a book of prose poetry, *Secret Heart*. She works as a secondary teacher and has a background in ecological science. Her latest collection is entitled *Western Line* (2011).

Ursula (Mary) Bethell (1874–1945) was born in England, raised in New Zealand, educated in England, and then returned to Christchurch in the 1920s. Bethell began writing aged fifty, with her first collection, *From a Garden in the Antipodes*, appearing in 1929. Her second collection, *Time and Place*, reflected the significance of both her garden and her close companion, Effie Pollen. Her *Collected Poems* was published posthumously in 1950 and again in 1985.

Peter Bland (1934–) was born in the United Kingdom. He is both a writer and an actor, and has published plays, several volumes of poetry, several children's books and a memoir. He was a founding member of Downstage Theatre in Wellington, and has moved between England and New Zealand throughout his life. His latest book is *Coming Ashore* (2011).

Jenny Bornholdt (1960–) lives in Wellington. She has produced eight volumes of poetry, and co-edited several anthologies. She has been appointed the Te Mata Estate New Zealand Poet Laureate, amongst numerous other honours. *The Rocky Shore* won the Poetry category at the Montana New Zealand Book Awards in 2009.

Charles Brasch (1909–1973) was born in Dunedin and attended Oxford University. He published six volumes of poetry (one appeared posthumously), and made a significant contribution to New Zealand literature as the founder of *Landfall*, which he edited for almost twenty years (1947–1966). Brasch was also a generous patron of the arts, establishing the Burns Fellowship at the University of Otago.

Diana Bridge (1942–) started to write poems while living in India in the 1990s. She has published several collections since the release of her first book, *Landscape with Lines,* in 1996. She has a PhD in Chinese poetry, has taught in the Chinese Department of Hong Kong University and has written on the China-based poems of Robin Hyde.

Bub Bridger (1924–2009) was a poet, actor and short story writer of Māori, Irish and English ancestry. She began writing at the age of fifty, after attending a writers' workshop run by historian Michael King at Victoria University. Her writing was widely anthologised and she published several poetry collections. She also wrote for television and broadcast radio.

Sarah Broom (1972–) is an Auckland-based writer. She has a D.Phil from the University of Oxford. Her book, *Contemporary British and Irish Poetry: An Introduction*, was published in 2006, and her first poetry collection, *Tigers at Awhitu*, debuted in 2010.

Diane Brown (1951–) is a poet, novelist and memoirist, and the coordinator and tutor for the Aoraki Polytechnic Creative Writing Course in Dunedin. She has published several volumes of poetry, and has won competitions in New Zealand and the UK. *Before the Divorce We Go To Disneyland* (1997) won the NZSA Jessie Mackay Best First Book of Poetry Award at the 1997 Montana New Zealand Book Awards.

James Brown (1966–) is a Wellington poet. His first poetry collection won the NZSA Jessie Mackay Award for Best First Book of Poetry. Since then, he has produced three more collections, received several writing fellowships and residencies, edited the literary magazine *Sport*, and had works in the annual *Best New Zealand Poems* selections.

Kate Camp (1972–) is a Wellington poet, prose writer and reviewer. Her first collection, *Unfamiliar Legends of the Stars*, won the NZSA Jessie Mackay Award for Best First Book of Poetry at the 1999 Montana New Zealand Book Awards. Her most recent collection, *The Mirror of Simple Annihilated Souls*, won the 2011 New Zealand Post Book Award for Poetry. She is the 2011 recipient of the Creative New Zealand Berlin Writers' Residency.

Alistair Te Ariki Campbell (1925–2009) was of Cook Islands and European descent. He was a graduate of Victoria University College and Wellington Teachers' College. As a prolific poet and novelist, Campbell received many honours, including a New Zealand Book Award for Poetry in 1982 and the Prime Minister's Award for Literary Achievement in Poetry in 2005. He was married to Fleur Adcock, and subsequently to Meg Anderson (Campbell).

Meg Campbell (1937–2007) was born and raised in Palmerston North and began to write in her forties. She published several collections of poetry and her writing appeared in a range of literary journals and magazines. She was married to the poet Alistair Te Ariki Campbell and lived on the Kapiti Coast.

Jill Chan (1973–) writes poetry and fiction. Her work has appeared in various New Zealand literary magazines and anthologies, both in print and online. She is the author of one novella and four collections of poetry, including *These Hands Are Not Ours* (2009), which won the Earl of Seacliff Poetry Prize.

Janet Charman (1954–) won the poetry category at the 2008 Montana New Zealand Book Awards with her sixth collection, *Cold Snack*. Charman is a featured poet on the New Zealand Electronic Poetry Centre website and was Literary Fellow at the University of Auckland in 1997.

Glenn Colquhoun (1964–) is a poet, children's writer and doctor. His first collection, *The Art of Walking Upright*, won the NZSA Jessie Mackay Best First Book of Poetry Award (2000). His third collection, *Playing God*, won the Montana New Zealand Book Award for Poetry, the Reader's Choice Award and achieved platinum sales. He has brought his latest collection, *Going South*, to life on stage with musical accompaniment.

Jen Crawford (1975–) was born in Taranaki and has lived in a number of North Island cities, as well as in the Philippines and Australia. Her current home is Singapore, where she teaches creative writing to university students. Her poetry publications include *Bad Appendix* (2008), *Napoleon Swings* (2010) and *Pop Riveter* (2011).

Wystan Curnow (1939–) was born in Christchurch and is the son of noted New Zealand poet Allen Curnow. A poet, essayist and art critic, Curnow gained his PhD from the University of Pennsylvania and is Emeritus Professor at the University of Auckland. He is the author of *Back in the USA*, *Cancer Daybook*, *Castor Bay* and *Modern Colours*.

Ruth Dallas (1919–2008) was born in Invercargill. She published numerous collections of poetry as well as eight novels for children. Her fifth collection, *Walking on the Snow*, received a New Zealand Book Award in 1977. Otago University awarded her the Burns Fellowship in 1968 and, a decade later, an honorary Doctor of Literature degree. She was made a CBE for her services to literature in 1989.

Lynn Davidson (1959–) writes fiction and poetry. Her work has appeared in journals and been broadcast on national radio. She has published several collections of poetry and a novel, *Ghost Net* (2003). She works as an educator and tutors in short fiction and poetry.

Eileen Duggan (1894–1972), of Irish ancestry, was born in Marlborough. She earned her living as a full-time writer for nearly fifty years, producing essays, criticism and journalism as well as several poetry books. She gained an MA (First Class Honours) in History from Victoria University, and in 1939 was elected to the International Gallery of Living Catholic Authors. She was made an honorary fellow of the Royal Society of Literature in 1943.

Lauris Edmond (1924–2000) was born and raised in Hawke's Bay. She had her first volume of poetry, *In Middle Air*, published at the age of fifty-one, and published about twenty further poetry books as well as a three-volume autobiography. She won the Commonwealth Poetry Prize in 1985, amongst many other honours, and was a founder of *New Zealand Books*. She edited *New Zealand Love Poems: An Oxford Anthology*.

Murray Edmond (1949–) was born in Hamilton. He is a poet, playwright, editor and critic who worked for a number of theatre companies during the 1970s and 1980s. He has published ten books of poetry, the latest of which is *Fool Moon* (2004), and edited three anthologies. Edmond teaches Drama at the University of Auckland and edits *Ka Mate Ka Ora: A New Zealand Journal of Poetry and Poetics*.

David Eggleton (1952–) was born in Auckland, grew up in both Fiji and New Zealand and is part Polynesian. He has published a number of poetry collections and books of prose, and edited two anthologies. *South Pacific Sunrise* was co-winner of the PEN Best First Book of Poetry Award in 1987. Eggleton is an award-winning book reviewer. He was the 1990 Burns Fellow at the University of Otago and is the current editor of *Landfall*.

Johanna Emeney (1974–) was born in Auckland and has an MA from Cambridge University. Her debut poetry collection, *Apple & Tree*, was published in 2011. She has published poems in numerous journals and magazines.

Riemke Ensing (1939–) was born in The Netherlands and has lived in New Zealand since 1951. She edited the first anthology of New Zealand women poets, *Private Gardens* (1977), and has published numerous collections of her own poetry, including *Talking Pictures: Selected Poems* (2000). She was the Buddle Findlay Sargeson Fellow in 2002.

A R D (Arthur Rex Dugard) Fairburn (1904–1957) was born in Auckland. As well as writing poetry, essays, reviews and criticism, he also painted, designed and printed fabrics, and was a critic of and lectured on art. His essays and reviews over twenty-five years form a mosaic of the intellectual life of New Zealand, and touch on most of the major issues of those years.

Fiona Farrell (1947–) lives in Otanerito on Banks Peninsula and has published three collections of poetry. The most recent, *The Pop-Up Book of Invasions*, was shortlisted for the 2008 Montana New Zealand Book Award for Poetry. She has received a number of honours, fellowships and awards, including The Prime Minister's Award for Literary Achievement (2007). In 2011 she published *The Broken Book*, a mix of prose and poetry.

Joan Fleming (1984–) lives in Golden Bay. After completing her MA in Creative Writing at Victoria University, she won the Biggs Poetry Prize in 2007 and also edited *Turbine* the same year. As well as tutoring for Massey, Joan has taught creative writing to both children and adults. Her debut collection, *The Same as Yes*, appeared in 2011.

Janet Frame (1924–2004) is best known as a novelist and for her three-volume autobiography, however she also produced a substantial number of poems. She published one collection, *The Pocket Mirror* (1967; 2004) in her lifetime, and her posthumous collection, *The Goose Bath*, won the 2007 Montana New Zealand Book Award for Poetry. At the bequest of her estate, The Janet Frame Trust now supports poets and fiction writers.

Rhian Gallagher (1961–) was born in Timaru. She completed a BA at London University and a Post-Graduate Diploma in Printing and Publishing at the London School of Printing. Her first collection, *Salt Water Creek* (2003), was short-listed for the Forward Prize for First Collection. She received the Janet Frame Literary Trust Award (2008) and has published a second collection, *Shift* (2011).

Denis Glover (1912–1980) was born in Dunedin. He was noted as a poet, printer and publisher and also as a pugilist, sailor and satirist. He founded the Caxton Press and co-founded *Landfall*, and his works include several of New Zealand's most widely anthologised poems. He was awarded an honorary doctorate of literature from Victoria University and elected President of Honour of the New Zealand Centre of PEN, the national association for authors.

Bernadette Hall (1945–) has published nine volumes of poetry, along with plays, essays and short fiction. She has held a number of residencies including the Rathcoola Residency in Ireland. She edited a collection of Joanna Margaret Paul's poems, *Like Love Poems*. She is a founding staff member of The Hagley Writers' Institute in Christchurch.

Michael Harlow (1937–), a poet and Jungian psychotherapist, of Greek and American-Ukraine lineage, was born in the United States and has lived in New Zealand since 1968. He has published critical prose, translations and seven books of poetry. He has been the Katherine Mansfield Fellow in France, and the Randell Cottage Writer in Residence. His latest collection, *The Tram Conductor's Blue Cap*, was published in 2009.

Dinah Hawken (1943–) was born in Hawera and studied physiotherapy, psychology and social work in New Zealand and the United States. Hawken has published six collections of poetry, including *It Has No Sound and Is Blue*, which won the Commonwealth Poetry Prize for Best First Time Published Poet in 1987. Her latest collection is *The Leaf-Ride* (2011).

Jeffrey Paparoa Holman (1947–) emigrated to New Zealand from London with his family in 1950. He grew up mainly on the West Coast and has a PhD in Cultural History from Canterbury University. He has published two poetry collections including *As Big as a Father* (2002), which was a finalist for the Montana New Zealand Book Awards Poetry Category (2003).

Ingrid Horrocks (1975–) writes poetry and creative non-fiction. She has a PhD from Princeton University and teaches Creative Writing at Massey University in Wellington. Her latest collection is entitled *Mapping the Distance* (2010).

Sam Hunt (1946–) was born in Auckland and travels the country reading his poems in schools, shows and taverns. He has published numerous bestselling poetry collections, including *Doubtless: New and Selected Poems* (2008). He has produced the semi-autobiographical, *Backroads Charting a Poet's Life* (2009), edited a selection of James K Baxter poems (2010) and produced *Chords & other Poems* (2011).

Robin Hyde (1906–1939) was born as Iris Wilkinson in Cape Town, South Africa, but grew up in Wellington. She studied at Victoria University before writing for the *Dominion* under the name 'Novita'. Hyde's brief writing life included ten books of poetry and prose. Two posthumous poetry publications, *Houses by the Sea* (1952) and *Young Knowledge: The Poems of Robin Hyde* (2003), have directed greater attention to her poems.

Kevin Ireland (1933–) lives in Devonport, Auckland. His output of poetry has been prodigious — the nineteenth volume appeared in 2009. Ireland's achievements also include five novels, two memoirs, an opera libretto and two book-length essays. He has received the Prime Minister's Award for Literary Achievement in Poetry (2004) amongst numerous other honours.

Anna Jackson (1967–) is a poet, essayist, editor, and fiction and academic writer, with a D.Phil from Oxford University. She has produced five volumes of poetry, and her work also appears in two collaborative collections. Born in Auckland, she now lives in Wellington, where she teaches at Victoria University. Her latest collection is entitled *Thicket* (2011).

Louis Johnson (1924–1988), a poet, editor, teacher and journalist, was born in Wellington. He established and edited the *New Zealand Poetry Yearbook* (1951–1964) and from 1963 he edited the *School Journal*. A prolific poet, with over fourteen published collections, he was a generous supporter of other writers — now acknowledged in the annual Louis Johnson New Writers Award.

Mike Johnson (1947–) lives on Waiheke Island. He is a poet, fiction writer and teacher. He has published numerous poetry collections, novels and novellas. He has won a number of awards and residencies including the University of Auckland Literary Fellowship. In 2007 he published *The Vertical Harp: Selected Poems of Li He*.

Stephanie Johnson (1961–) is the author of two collections of poetry, *The Bleeding Ballerina* and *Moody Bitch*, as well as three collections of short stories and seven novels. Her novel *The Shag Incident* won the Montana Medal for Fiction in 2002. Stephanie has won the Bruce Mason Playwrights Award and Katherine Mansfield Fellowship.

Andrew Johnston (1963–) was born in Upper Hutt and now lives in France, where he is an editor for the *International Herald Tribune*. He has produced four more poetry books since his award-winning debut, *How to Talk*. He was the 2007 JD Stout Fellow at Victoria University of Wellington, edited *Moonlight: New Zealand poems on death and dying* (2008) and co-edited *Twenty Contemporary New Zealand Poets* (2009).

Kapka Kassabova (1973–) is a Bulgarian poet, travel writer and novelist who has lived in New Zealand, Europe and the UK. She has published four poetry collections, three novels, a travel memoir and a book on the tango. Her awards include the NZSA Jessie Mackay Award for Best First Book of Poetry and the Commonwealth Writers' Prize for Best First Novel (South-East Asia and South Pacific).

Jan Kemp (1949–) is a poet and short-story writer. She began performing with the *Freed* group in the late 1960s and toured New Zealand in the 1970s in the 'Gang of Four' — with Sam Hunt, Alistair Campbell and Hone Tuwhare. She is co-editor of three New Zealand CD poetry anthologies (2006–08), has published over six volumes of poetry and now lives outside Frankfurt am Main in Germany.

Anne Kennedy (1959–) is an award-winning writer who currently teaches at the University of Hawai'i. She has published fiction — two novels, a novella and short fiction — as well as two volumes of poetry. *Sing-Song* won the Montana New Zealand Book Award for Poetry (2004) and her second collection was shortlisted two years later.

Fiona Kidman (1940–) is well known as a short-story writer and novelist and has published over twenty books, including five poetry collections. Her most recent volume, *Where Your Left Hand Rests*, appeared in 2010. She has received numerous honours and awards and was named Dame Companion of the New Zealand Order of Merit for her services to literature. She is the President of Honour for the New Zealand Book Council.

Richard Langston (1959–) grew up in Dunedin. His books of poetry are *Boy* (2003), *Henry, Come See the Blue* (2005), *The Newspaper Poems* (2007), and *The Trouble Lamp* (2009). He is working on a new book, and can be heard reading his poems on Afternoons on Radio New Zealand National.

Michele Leggott (1956–) is an award-winning poet, academic, essayist and editor. She coordinates the New Zealand Electronic Poetry Centre with Brian Flaherty at the University of Auckland. Her debut collection, *Like This?*, won PEN Best First Book of Poetry and *DIA* won the New Zealand Book Award for Poetry (1994). From 2007–2009 she was New Zealand Poet Laureate. She is Professor of English at the University of Auckland.

Renee Liang (1973–) is a poet, playwright, fiction writer and paediatrician who lives in Auckland. She has published several poetry chapbooks, her work has appeared in a number of online and print literary journals, and she has had three plays produced. She was named a Sir Peter Blake Emerging Leader in 2010 and is involved in community projects.

Anna Livesey (1979–) was born and raised in Wellington and has an MA in Creative Writing from Victoria University. She has won the Macmillan Brown Prize on two occasions and was the Schaeffer Fellow at the Iowa Writers' Workshop (2003). She has published two collections of poetry, the latest of which is entitled *Moonmen* (2010).

Iain Lonie (1932–1988), a poet and academic, lectured in Classics at Otago University. He published six collections of poetry including the posthumous collection, *Winter Walking at Morning* (1991).

Rachel McAlpine (1940–) is a poet, novelist and playwright. Her first collection of poetry, *Lament for Ariadne*, was published in 1975. She has since published numerous other collections and written several plays and novels. Her non-fiction work includes ESOL textbooks, books about writing and writers, and how to write for the web.

Cilla McQueen (1949–) was raised in Birmingham and came to New Zealand in 1953. She has published eleven poetry collections, two of which have won New Zealand Book Awards. She has held literary fellowships in several countries, and has lived in Bluff for some years. She was New Zealand Poet Laureate from 2009–2011 and has received other key awards.

Bill Manhire (1946–) was born in Invercargill. Winner of five prestigious New Zealand awards for his poetry, he was the first Te Mata Estate New Zealand Poet Laureate. Among his many honours, he received the

Prime Minister's Award for Literary Achievement in Poetry (2007). He directs the International Institute of Modern Letters at Victoria University, and has published numerous collections of poetry, short stories and essays, and has edited several anthologies. His latest collection is *Victims of Lightning* (2010).

Selina Tusitala Marsh (1971–) was born in Auckland and is of Samoan, Tuvulu, English and French descent. She was the first Pacific Islander to gain a PhD in English from the University of Auckland, where she now teaches. Her debut collection, *Fast Talking PI*, won Best First Book at the New Zealand Book Awards (2010). She established and coordinates Pasifika Poetry, an online sister site of the New Zealand Electronic Poetry Centre.

Owen Marshall (1941–), chiefly a prose writer, has written or edited numerous books including two poetry collections. He has held the Katherine Mansfield Memorial Fellowship in France, and has received numerous honours, awards and fellowships for his writing. In 2000 he became an Officer of the New Zealand Order of Merit (ONZM) for services to literature. His latest poetry collection is entitled *Sleepwalking in Antarctica* (2010).

Karlo Mila (1974–) is of Tongan, Samoan and Palagi descent and lives in Palmerston North. Her debut collection, *Dream Fish Floating*, won the NZSA Jessie Mackay Award for Best First Book of Poetry in 2006. Her most recent collection, *A Well Written Body*, was published in 2008. She is a member of the Polynation performance group.

David Mitchell (1940–2011) was born in Wellington. His first collection of poems, *Pipe Dreams in Ponsonby*, was published in 1972 and although he wrote and performed extensively, his next book, *Steal Away Boy: Selected Poems of David Mitchell*, did not appear until 2010. Mitchell founded Auckland's Poetry Live! in 1980 and ran it for three years. He completed a Bachelor of Arts from Victoria University in 2002.

Emma Neale (1969–) lives in Dunedin and has a PhD from London's University College. She has published three collections of poetry, four novels and in 2008 edited *Swings and Roundabouts: Poems on Parenthood*. Neale is the 2012 Robert Burns Fellow at Otago University and won The Kathleen Grattan Award for Poetry in 2011.

James Norcliffe (1946–) is an editor, poet and fiction writer. He has published six collections of poetry, a collection of short stories and several novels for young people. He is poetry editor for *Takahe* magazine and the *Christchurch Press*, and co-edits the annual *Re-Draft* anthologies of young writing.

Gregory O'Brien (1961–) is a prolific poet, noted artist, curator, art writer, essayist, teacher and anthologist. He has published eight poetry collections, a novel, a novella and numerous award-winning works of non-fiction. Three of his poems appear online in the annual *Best New Zealand Poems* collections. He co-edited the anthology of New Zealand love poems, *My Heart Goes Swimming*, with Jenny Bornholdt.

Bob Orr (1949–) was born in Hamilton and is now based in Auckland, where he works as a boatman on the Waitemata Harbour. Orr was one of the poets strongly associated in the 1970s with *Freed* magazine and Arthur Baysting's *The Young New Zealand Poets*. He has published over seven collections of poetry, most recently *Calypso* (2008).

Joanna Margaret Paul (1945–2003) was born in Hamilton. She was a painter, poet and experimental filmmaker. She published several collections of poetry, but the full scope of her poetry was revealed posthumously in *Like Love Poems*, edited by Bernadette Hall. Her debut poetry collection *IMOGEN* was awarded the PEN Best First Book Award for Poetry in 1978.

Kiri Piahana-Wong (1977–) is of Māori, Chinese and English ancestry. Her work has been widely published in journals and anthologies in New Zealand and Australia. She is also a performance poet, and an MC at Poetry Live, New Zealand's longest-running live poetry venue. She lives on Auckland's North Shore.

Vivienne Plumb (1955–) is an actor, playwright and fiction writer as well as a poet. She has published seven poetry collections and has held several residencies, including the 2006 Massey University writers' residency and one in 2004 at the University of Iowa. She is completing a Doctorate in Creative Arts and divides her time between Sydney and Auckland.

Brian Potiki (1953–), of Kāi Tāhu, Kati Māmoe origins, is a poet, playwright, scriptwriter, songwriter and performer. His poems have been published in numerous magazines and anthologies, and in his debut collection, *Aotearoa* (2003). He has toured extensively, performing and running workshops as 'The Travelling Tuataras' with his partner, Jill Walker.

Jenny Powell (1960–) is a poet and teacher based in Dunedin. She is a graduate of John Dolan's poetry class at Otago University, and has published five poetry collections. These include two collaborative works, *Double Jointed* with ten poets (2003) and *Locating the Madonna* with Anna Jackson (2004).

Joanna Preston (1972–) was born in Sydney and spent her childhood in outback New South Wales. She has an MPhil in Creative Writing from the University of Glamorgan, and moved to Christchurch in 1994. Her award-winning poems have been widely published in New Zealand and internationally. In 2008 she was the inaugural winner of The Kathleen Grattan Award for Poetry, and published *The Summer King*.

Chris Price (1962–) is a poet, editor and musician. Her first poetry collection, *Husk*, was the NZSA Jessie Mackay Best First Book of Poetry winner (2002), and her mixed-genre work *Brief Lives* (2006) was shortlisted in the biography category. She has won several residencies including the Katherine Mansfield Memorial Fellowship (2011). She teaches Creative Writing at Victoria University's International Institute of Modern Letters in Wellington.

John Pahiatau Pule (1962–) is a poet, novelist and artist. He was born in Liku, Niue, and arrived in New Zealand in 1964. He began writing in the 1980s after reading the work of Hone Tuwhare and has published several poetry collections. There are strong connections between his painting and his poetry. He lives in Auckland.

Sarah Quigley (1967–) was born in Christchurch and is an award-winning novelist, critic and columnist. She holds a D.Phil. in Literature from the University of Oxford and in 1998 won the Buddle Findlay Sargeson Fellowship. She has published four novels, a collection of short fiction, a creative writing manual, and two poetry collections. In 2000 she won the inaugural Creative New Zealand Berlin Residency. She lives in Berlin.

Helen Rickerby (1974–) lives in Wellington. Her most recent book of poetry is *My Iron Spine* (2008), a collection of biographical and autobiographical poems. She is co-managing editor of *JAAM* literary magazine, and runs a small publishing company, Seraph Press.

Harry Ricketts (1950–) works as Associate Professor of English at Victoria University. He is a biographer, co-editor of *New Zealand Books*, an essayist, anthologist and a poet with six collections to his name. He grew up in England, Malaysia and Hong Kong, and migrated to New Zealand in 1981.

Jack Ross (1962–) was born in Auckland. His publications include three novels, two books of short fiction, and several volumes of poetry. He edited, with Jan Kemp, the trilogy of audio and text anthologies *Classic, Contemporary and New New Zealand Poets in Performance* (2006–08). He teaches Academic and Creative Writing at Massey University's Albany campus.

Iain Sharp (1953–) is a poet, columnist, reviewer and critic. He has published several collections of poetry as well as non-fiction, and is a practised performer of his poetry. His non-fiction titles include a history of the Spirit of Adventure Trust, a book about the rare books in the Auckland City Library collection, and a major biography of Charles Heaphy.

Keith Sinclair (1922–1993) was born in Auckland. He was a historian, biographer and poet. His non-fiction books included the bestselling *History of New Zealand* and several groundbreaking biographies. He published five volumes of poetry.

Anna Smaill (1979–) is a poet with a background in English literature and music performance. Her first collection, *The Violinist in Spring* (2006), was listed as one of the year's best books in the *New Zealand Listener*. Her poems have been widely published in journals and magazines, including *Best New Zealand Poems* in both 2002 and 2005.

Elizabeth Smither (1941–) lives in Taranaki and has produced seventeen volumes of poetry as well as five novels and five short-story collections. Among many other honours, Smither was awarded the Te Mata

Estate New Zealand Poet Laureate in 2002 and the Prime Minister's Award for Literary Achievement in Poetry (2008). Her latest work, *The Commonplace Book*, is a writer's journey through quotations.

Charles Spear (1910–1985) was born in Owaka, South Otago. He published a number of poems in New Zealand literary journals. Caxton Press published his only collection of poetry, *Twopence Coloured*, in 1952. Holloway Press reissued this collection, along with images by Tony Lane and previously unpublished poems, in 2007.

Mary Stanley (1919–1980) was a poet whose output was limited to a particular period of her life. She won the Jessie Mackay Memorial Award of 1945 with three of her earliest poems. In 1951, she published her sole collection, *Starveling Year*.

C K (Christian Karlson) Stead (1932–) is a poet, novelist and critic. He retired as Professor of English at the University of Auckland in 1986 to devote himself to writing full time. His sixteen volumes of poetry include *Collected Poems: 1955–2000* which won the reference and anthology category of the Montana New Zealand Book Awards (2009). His numerous honours include the Prime Minister's Award for Achievement in Literary Fiction (2009).

Michael Steven (1977–) was born in Auckland. His books include *Bartering Lines*, and *Daybook Fragments*.

J C (Jacqueline Cecilia) Sturm (1927–2009), a poet and short-story writer, was born in Opunake and was of Taranaki Māori descent. One of the first Māori women to gain a degree, she gained an MA (First Class Honours) in Philosophy from Victoria University. She wrote several poetry collections including the award-winning *Dedications*. In 2003, she received an honorary doctorate from Victoria University. She was married to the poet James K Baxter.

Robert Sullivan (1967–) is a poet of Kāi Tāhu, Ngāpuhi, Ngāti Raukawa and Irish descent. He is currently Head of the School of Creative Writing at the Manukau Institute of Technology. He has published seven books of poetry, two works of fiction and edited several poetry anthologies. He has won several New Zealand literary awards, including PEN Best First Book Award for Poetry for *Jazz Waiata* (1991).

Apirana Taylor (1955–) was born in Wellington and is of Te Whānau ō Apanui, Ngāti Porou, and Ngāti Ruanui and Pākehā descent. Taylor has published five volumes of poetry, short stories, a novel, plays and criticism. He was actively involved in the Māori theatre co-operative Te Ohu Whakaari. He was awarded fellowships in writing from Massey University (1996) and the University of Canterbury (2002).

Chris Tse (1982–) is a Wellington writer, actor, musician and occasional filmmaker. He has completed an MA in Creative Writing at Victoria University. His poetry has appeared in various journals and he is a feature poet in *AUP New Poets 4*

Brian Turner (1944–) is a prolific poet and non-fiction writer. His first book, *Ladders of Rain*, won the Commonwealth Poetry Prize in 1979 and he has won the New Zealand Book Award for Poetry in 1992 and in 2010. He was appointed Te Mata Estate New Zealand Poet Laureate in 2003. His latest collection is *Taking Off* (2011). He lives in Central Otago.

Hone Tuwhare (1922–2008) was of Ngāpuhi descent. His debut collection, *No Ordinary Sun*, became one of New Zealand's best-selling poetry collections (1964). He published seventeen further volumes, two of which won New Zealand Book Awards. He was Te Mata Estate New Zealand Poet Laureate from 1999–2001. Tuwhare received two honorary doctorates in literature and won the inaugural Prime Minister's Award for Literary Achievement in Poetry (2003).

Ian Wedde (1946–) has published numerous books of poetry, as well as novels, essays and art criticism. He co-edited *The Penguin Book of New Zealand Verse* (1985). His awards include the Katherine Mansfield Memorial Fellowship in 2005, a New Zealand Arts Foundation Laureateship in 2006, and a Distinguished Alumni Award from the University of Auckland in 2007. He is the New Zealand Poet Laureate from 2011–2013.

Albert Wendt (1939–) was born in Apia, Samoa. He gained an MA from Victoria University and has since received many other honours. Wendt was pro-vice chancellor at the University of the South Pacific in Fiji and then Professor of English at the University of Auckland. He has published four volumes of poetry, a play, and numerous novels and short-story collections. His verse novel, *The Adventures of Vela*, won the Commonwealth Writers Prize for the Asia Pacific Region in 2010. He lives in Auckland.

Virginia Were (1960–) lives in Auckland. She is a poet, fiction writer and critic. She has published two collections of poetry and is the editor of *Art News New Zealand*.

Alison Wong (1960–) is a third-generation Chinese New Zealander with a BSc in Mathematics. She now lives in Australia. She has held two writing fellowships, produced two poetry collections, and also written fiction. Her first novel, *As the Earth Turns Silver* (2009), was Fiction Award winner at the 2010 New Zealand Post Book Awards, while *Cup* was shortlisted for the NZSA Jessie Mackay Best First Book Award for Poetry (2007).

Sue Wootton (1961–) was the 2008 Robert Burns Fellow at Otago University and her second collection of poetry, *Magnetic South*, was published the same year. She has won awards for her poetry, and had a poem selected for *Best New Zealand Poems 2004*. Her latest collection is entitled *By Birdlight* (2011).

Sonja Yelich (1965–) lives in Auckland and is of Dalmatian descent. She trained as a teacher and studied literature at the University of Auckland. After publication in the *AUP New Poets* series, her first solo collection, *Clung*, won the NZSA Jessie Mackay

Best First Book Award for Poetry (2005). Her second collection, *Get Some*, was a finalist in the Montana New Zealand Book Awards (2008). She won the Buddle Findlay Sargeson Fellowship in 2010.

Artist biographies

Dick Frizzell — 'e', page 134 — lives and works in the Hawke's Bay. He was born in Auckland in 1943 and attended the University of Canterbury School of Fine Arts from 1960 to 1963, where he studied under artists such as Rudi Gopas and Russell Clark. As well as in the visual arts, he has worked in advertising and as a commercial artist, animator and illustrator. His work often portrays an ironic sense of humour and he has become an established figure in New Zealand's visual culture. He is the author of *Dick Frizzell: The Painter* (2009) and an appraisal of favourite New Zealand paintings in *It's All About the Image* (2011).

Michael Hight — 'a', page 158 and endpapers and jacketflaps — was born in Stratford, Taranaki, in 1961. He gained a Bachelor of Social Science at Waikato University, and from 1984–87 lived and painted in London. His interest in beehives, which he uses as a metaphor in many of his realist and abstract paintings, dates from the mid-1990s. Hight has worked full-time as an artist since 2001, and now lives and works in Auckland. His work is held in many major collections in New Zealand.

Sam Mitchell — 'r', page 182 — was born in Colorado Springs in the United States, and moved to New Zealand with her family as a young girl. She studied at Elam School of Fine Arts, where she completed a BFA in 1998 and an MFA in 2000. In 2010 she won the Paramount Prize in the Wallace Art Awards, which led to a six-month residency at the International Studio and Curatorial Program in New York. Her work reflects her fascination with the techniques of cartooning and tattooing, which she often combines to create incongruous and thought-provoking images.

Gregory O'Brien — 'd', page 31 — is a poet, anthologist, curator and art critic, as well as a painter. Born in Matamata, he trained and worked as a journalist before returning to study for a BA in Art History and English at the University of Auckland, graduating in 1984. After a two-year stint working as arts editor of a television programme, he spent a number of years curating major exhibitions at Wellington City Gallery (1997–2009). He has contributed to numerous art catalogues and his art publications include the award-winning *Back and Beyond; New Zealand Art for the Young and the Curious* (2008). In 2011 he published books on the painter Euan Macleod and the artist Graham Percy. There are strong links between his poetry and his painting.

Reuben Paterson (Ngāti Rangitihi and Tuhoe) — 'r', page 89 (letter design by Mark Remoquillo) — lives and works in Auckland, where he was born in 1973. He studied at Elam School of Fine Arts, graduating in 1997. After being awarded the Moët and Chandon Fellowship to France, he remained in Europe for a further two years, travelling widely and living in England. He has also lived and worked in Greece. Paterson has represented New Zealand at a number of events, including the 8th Festival of Pacific Arts Biennale d'Art Contemporain (2000), the Prague International Biennale of Contemporary Art (2005) and the 17th Biennale of Sydney (2010).

Johanna Pegler — 'e', page 47 — was born in Auckland in 1965. She graduated from Elam School of Fine Arts in 1987, and after a period travelling and working in the South Island in the early nineties she settled in Waikawau Bay, at the tip of the Coromandel Peninsula. In 2004 she moved to Whanganui, initially as artist in residence at Tylee Cottage, and in 2009 was artist in residence at Awhitu Regional Park, on the shores of the Manukau Harbour. She is known particularly for her idiosyncratic landscapes.

John Pule — 'h', page 109 — was born in 1962 in Liku, Niue, but when he was two his family moved to Auckland, where he lives and works today. Visits to Niue as an adult inspired an interest in the island's history and mythology, and his paintings often include references to hiapo, the Niuean tapa cloth, and other symbols. A self-taught artist, he is a poet and writer as well as a painter and printmaker, often combining the different forms. His work has been included in two Asia-Pacific Triennials at the Queensland Art Gallery, and in 2004 it also formed part of *Paradise Now!* at the Asia Society in New York. He was a 2004 Arts Foundation of New Zealand Laureate.

John Reynolds — 't', page 207 — lives and works in Auckland, where he was born in 1956. Since graduating from Elam School of Fine Arts in 1978 he has won a number of awards, including the Montana Lindauer Award in 1988 and the VisaGold Award in 1994, and he was a finalist in the Wallace Art Awards in both 2002 and 2008. In 2006 his work *Clouds* was featured at the *Zones of Contact* Sydney Biennale. He works in a range of forms, and has collaborated with other artists such as the painter Ralph Hotere and the late poet Leigh Davis.

Emily Wolfe — 'a', page 66 — was born in Auckland and studied at Elam from 1993–96, graduating with a BFA. In 1998 she began studies at the Slade School of Fine Art in London, winning a Ryoichi Sasakawa Scholarship from Massey University in 1999, and completing her Master's degree in 2000. In 2006 she was selected for the John Moores Painting Prize at the Walker Art Gallery in Liverpool, and in 2009 she was included in the painting exhibition East End Academy at the Whitechapel Gallery in London. She continues to be based in London, exhibiting throughout England, in Belgium and in New Zealand, and she travels between this country and the northern hemisphere frequently.

About the editor

Paula Green (1955–) was born in Auckland. She graduated from Wellington Teachers College and from the University of Auckland (MA Hons, PhD Italian). She has published seven poetry collections, including two for children, and several storybooks including *Aunt Concertina and her Niece Evalina* (2009). With Harry Ricketts she co-edited *99 Ways into New Zealand Poetry*, which was shortlisted for the 2011 New Zealand Post Book Awards Non-fiction category. She was the 2005 University of Auckland Literary Fellow and curated Poetry on the Pavement for the Auckland City Council in the same year. She edited *Best New Zealand Poems 2007*. She is a poetry and fiction reviewer for *The New Zealand Herald*.

Index of titles and poets

'6 The Eternal Sunshine of the Spotless Mind' 212

'A Consort of Flower Parts' 112
'A Girl's Song' 168
'A Late Honeymoon' 70
'A Letter' 94
'A Lightning Tree' 88
'A Lullaby' 167
'A new plateau song' 96
Adcock, Fleur 208, 236
'After Apollinaire' 104
Andrews, Angela 25, 236
'Apartment' 24
'Arohanui' 18
'As big as a father' 98
'At Scorching Bay' 197
'At the Beginning of Love' 64
'At your visit' 146
'Audrey' 27
'August' 209
'Aunty Huia' 192

Baker, Hinemoana 78, 236
'Barbara' 198
Barford, Serie 116, 237
Barnett, Sarah Jane 22, 237
Baxter, James K 32, 183, 237

'Bear Dance' 56
Beautrais, Airini 26, 29, 237
'because' 83
'Before I Get into Sleep with You' 75
Bethell, Ursula 169, 238
'Between' 144
'Billet-doux' 48
'Birdsong' 118
Bland, Peter 56, 139, 157, 238
Bornholdt, Jenny 20, 126, 194, 238
'Bouquet of Dead Flowers' 176
Brasch, Charles 172, 238
Bridge, Diana 77, 239
Bridger, Bub 35, 239
'Brightness' 45
Broom, Sarah 83, 118, 239
Brown, Diane 33, 239
Brown, James 142, 154, 240
'[but you…]' 28

'Calculations' 122
Camp, Kate 152, 240
Campbell, Alistair Te Ariki 67, 240
Campbell, Meg 211, 240
'Cassino *Città Martire*' 174
'Catch' 241

— 267 —

Chan, Jill 133, 241
'Change' 110
Charman, Janet 128, 148, 241
'Cherries' 204
'Child' 65
Colquhoun, Glenn 180, 192, 241
'Coming and Going' 141
Crawford, Jen 145, 241
Curnow, Wystan 28, 242

Dallas, Ruth 168, 242
Davidson, Lynn 196, 242
'dear heart' 217
'December' 150
'Deserts, for instance' 166
'dia' (extract) 106
'Dog's body' 151
'Dream' 17
Duggan, Eileen 161, 242

Edmond, Lauris 90, 243
Edmond, Murray 224, 243
Eggleton, David 176, 243
'Embrace' 76
Emeney, Johanna 52, 243
'Ending and going home' 126
Ensing, Riemke 124, 244

Fairburn, A R D 110, 244
Farrell, Fiona 38, 111, 244
Fleming, Joan 103, 202, 244
'Fontanello' 86
'For the father of my children' 58
'For Thee' 223
'Found Again' 116
Frame, Janet 65, 75, 245
'Free fall' 140

Gallagher, Rhian 144, 147, 245
'Glenburn' 34
Glover, Denis 45, 245

'grahams beach, bach' 54
'Great Full Moon, Lowering Behind the Black Hill' 62
Green, Paula 34

Hall, Bernadette 36, 82, 197, 245
Harlow, Michael 48, 246
Hawken, Dinah 30, 107, 201, 246
'He Waiata mo Te Kare' 183
'His eyes' 79
Holman, Jeffrey Paparoa 98, 246
'Homage' 169
Horrocks, Ingrid 84, 246
Hunt, Sam 96, 123, 247
'Husband and Wife Talk Without Talking at a Difficult Dinner Party' 103
'Husband to Wife' 61
Hyde, Robin 76, 247

'I love peaches' 80
'I Love Those Photos' 213
'If She Hadn't Been There' 69
'Inesilla' 46
'Inventing You' 100
'In Your Presence' (extract) 172
Ireland, Kevin 60, 100, 247

Jackson, Anna 86, 108, 248
'jill' 216
Johnson, Louis 141, 248
Johnson, Mike 135, 248
Johnson, Stephanie 209, 248
Johnston, Andrew 92, 249

Kassabova, Kapka 122, 199, 249
'keeping warm' 40
Kemp, Jan 74, 249
Kennedy, Anne 220, 249
Kidman, Fiona 72, 250

Langston, Richard 179, 250
Leggott, Michele 40, 106, 217, 250
'Lemon Tree' 162
'Let's be honest here' 222
'Letter home' 123
Liang, Renee 204, 250
'Life eternal' 77
'light' 191
Livesey, Anna 62, 251
Lonie, Iain 70, 251
'Love Affair' 124
'Love by Candlelight' 49
'Love in the Dark Country' 199
'Love in the Early Winter' 19
'Love in the Jam-maker's Mansion' 195
'Love poem' 23
'Love Poem for a Love a Long Time Ago' 26
'Love poem for David' 130
'Love Poem for the Tauherenikau River' 29
'Love Song' 44
'lovesong' 82
'Lyric' 190

McAlpine, Rachel 44, 251
McQueen, Cilla 88, 102, 251
'Makara' 202
Manhire, Bill 46, 137, 167, 251
Marsh, Selina Tusitala 130, 252
Marshall, Owen 162, 252
Mila, Karlo 58, 159, 252
Mitchell, David 94, 253
'Mute song' 152
'My Mother Dances' 129
'My Mother's Voice' 84

Neale, Emma 81, 206, 253
'Newborn' 206
Norcliffe, James 195, 253

O'Brien, Gregory 23, 112, 253
'Of books and bookcases' 177
'On a Son Returned to New Zealand' 208
Orr, Bob 198, 254

Paul, Joanna Margaret 79, 87, 146, 254
Piahana-Wong, Kiri 177, 254
'Picnic at Darkness Falls' 154
Plumb, Vivienne 80, 213, 254
'Poem for Kereihi' 63
'Portland Crescent' 163
Potiki, Brian 216, 255
Powell, Jenny 19, 85, 255
Preston, Joanna 214, 255
Price, Chris 151, 255
'Puer Natus' 91
Pule, John Puhiatau 164, 256
'Puriri' 74

'Quarantine Island' 95
Quigley, Sarah 150, 256

'Remembering Summer' 156
'Returned Memory' 107
Rickerby, Helen 212, 256
Ricketts, Harry 95, 140, 256
Ross, Jack 55, 104, 256
'Ruby's heirloom dress' 37

'See what a little moonlight can do to you?' 138
'Seven wishes' 111
Sharp, Iain 127, 257
'She and Her First Best Boyfriend' 201
'Silly' 211
Sinclair, Keith 171, 257
Smaill, Anna 163, 257
Smither, Elizabeth 37, 64, 257

'Son' 24
Spear, Charles 27, 258
Stanley, Mary 49, 91, 258
Stead, C K 53, 258
Steven, Michael 190, 258
'Still Life' 87
Sturm, J C 121, 222, 259
Sullivan, Robert 18, 174, 259

'talk about a tonic' 33
Taylor, Apirana 120, 259
'Tell me you're waiting' 139
'The Apple Picker' 22
'The Beach House' 32
'The Bicycle' 142
'the bird' 180
'The Bond Of Time: An Epic Love Poem' (extract) 164
'The castle' 38
'The Dance' 147
'The Fire is Lovely' 179
'The gift' 157
'The Grin' 171
'The Inner Life' 194
'The Language of Bluff' 102
'The Messenger' 214
'The Miracle' 55
'The nervous public speaker' 90
'The ngaio tree' 72
'The photograph' 125
'The Sounds' 92
'The Tides Run Up the Wairau' 161
'The Time of the Giants' (extract) 220
'The treehouse' 108
'The Verb to Give' 30
'The Voyage' 137
'The Wish' 60
'This is Love' 159
'Time of Day' 78

'Tipple Over Tail' 52
'to Pru' 120
'To Utopias' 50
'Traveller overdue' 81
'Treasure Hunt' (extract) 125
'Tryst' 200
Tse, Chris 61, 259
Turner, Brian 17, 69, 156, 166, 260
Tuwhare, Hone 63, 138, 223, 260
'Twelve Words Spoken by a Poem' 133

'Urgently' 121

'viaduct' 145

'warm loaf' 128
'Watching the Motorway by Moonlight' 127
Wedde, Ian 50, 260
'Wedding song' 20
'wedding song' 36
Wendt, Albert 129, 260
Were, Virginia 24, 261
'White Gold' 85
'Wide open spaces' 196
'Wild Daisies' 35
Wong, Alison 125, 191, 261
Wootton, Sue 200, 261
'Words and Roses' from 'Cages For the Wind' 67

Yelich, Sonja 54, 261
'You' 53
'you are a hot -concentrate' 148

creative nz
ARTS COUNCIL OF NEW ZEALAND TOI AOTEAROA

The assistance of Creative New Zealand is gratefully acknowledged by the publisher.

A GODWIT BOOK published by Random House New Zealand,
18 Poland Road, Glenfield, Auckland, New Zealand

For more information about our titles go to www.randomhouse.co.nz

A catalogue record for this book is available from the National Library of New Zealand

Random House New Zealand is part of the Random House Group
New York   London   Sydney   Auckland   Delhi   Johannesburg

First published 2012

© 2012 introduction text, Paula Green; poems as credited on pages 227–235; cover and inside images as credited on pages 262–265

The moral rights of the author have been asserted

ISBN 978 1 86979 762 1

This book is copyright. Except for the purposes of fair reviewing no part of this publication may be reproduced or transmitted in any form or by any means, electronic or mechanical, including photocopying, recording or any information storage and retrieval system, without permission in writing from the publisher.

Design: Megan van Staden
Printed in China by Everbest Printing Co Ltd